Gardening can be frustrating. It can be exhilarating. It brings up all sorts of questions and mixed emotions. Where do you start? What does this tool do? Why won't this plant grow? The gardening world is also full of myths. You've heard all about the horrors of clay soils, about plants that seem to grow a mile a minute, or the gloom-laden assertions that nothing grows well in pots, and that nothing at all will grow in shade. And you think to yourself – why bother? Gardening must be for other people, people who know what they're doing, with plenty of time, loads of money and a place in the country.

Below *Verbena bonariensis* is a favourite of mine – it's majestic, beautiful and, very importantly, doesn't demand too much maintenance.

But hold on, wait a minute – don't throw the book away just yet! This isn't the whole story. I'm a relative youngster in the garden, and though I've been gardening both professionally and at home for over ten years now, I still get crazy feelings about it. Sometimes I get a rush of sheer pleasure, so that I yell at the top of my voice and run round rubbing my hands and chortling like a lunatic! And sometimes I feel the complete opposite: bitter disappointment verging on insane resentment.

It's a fact – gardens can drive you mad; maybe they ought to carry a health warning. And if you live in a city these feelings are likely to be more pronounced, what with the noise, the pollution and the lack of privacy. You think you must have the most overgrown garden, the most cramped balcony, the most exposed roof terrace or the dullest window box in the history of the world. Surely, nothing on earth will transform your space to make it look like the immaculate gardens pictured in the kind of books that live on posh people's coffee tables?

But then again, we all know such-and-such from number 52 who's made a nice little urban space for themselves. So how did they do it? Possibly they got a contractor who charged them a fortune (at least, we'd like to think they did). Or maybe they just took the plunge, did a little research, and had a go. Real gardening is getting-your-hands-dirty creative and there is nobody on earth who can't do it. It's in our genes.

I hope that through this book I can inspire and help you, give you the basic knowledge to set you on your way, dish out a few shortcuts and – most important of all – show you that gardening is fun!

GETTING YOUR HANDS DIRTY

Your urban space may be so tiny you wonder what on earth you can do with it. Don't worry – everyone feels like that. My garden's the size of a shoebox. In fact, it's the size of a shoebox for kids' trainers. Strictly speaking, it's not even a garden, it's a balcony with views of other people's balconies. So why is my little high-rise back yard an all-consuming passion? I wish I knew! Gardens can get to you. But help is at hand and gardening is one area where a little bit of knowledge and a hands-on approach can go a long, long way.

Attitudes to gardening vary widely. For some, gardening is a chore, something which has to be done – like the Sunday housework or the washing up. Others, like some of my friends, really don't know where to start; they feel shy about asking around. And most of the rest are just plain lazy. At various times you'll find me in each camp. I am, in fact, one of the laziest gardeners around as there is always so much other stuff to do. I don't want a labour-intensive garden which requires daily attention. I want to do the cool jobs – the planting and pruning, for instance, not the weeding. And I want to see the finished results now, not in five years' time. Urban gardener? Impatient gardener, more like! I want to have friends round, eat tasty food in a garden illuminated with soft, sexy lighting; I don't want to be breaking my back digging and weeding every weekend.

Who was it said gardening has to be boring – another chore you have to do, like washing and ironing? I felt just the same once, and now I want to pull you out of the gardening blues and resurrect your interest, simply because I know it can be done. Your's is an urban paradise just waiting to happen. Get stuck in and make it so! Above all else, gardening should be enjoyable. A time when you're outside, not stuck in a stuffy office or channel-hopping bored in front of the telly. Your garden should be a place to unwind, to chill out, but also somewhere you can really explore your creative side. I always look at the time spent on my balcony as 'quiet time' – time on my own, relaxing, talking to my plants over a glass of wine.

It's true that some parts of gardening are hard work: the initial clearing of the site, for example. And yes, it may drive you, like me, to get frustrated now and then, and childishly throw your tools around, like the golfer who has missed the easiest putt. It's at times like these I have to remind myself that all the hard work is going to give me fantastic results. I will definitely reap what I sow – and more.

Left Believe me, gardening can drive you nuts! But it can also be mind-blowingly rewarding – particularly when it all comes together.
Below Whether you like architectural green plants, or flowers such as echinacea, your little patch of space will be a source of pleasure (and frustration!).

Far right Planting is the ideal therapy for city dwellers with a hectic and stressful lifestyle. It puts you in touch with nature and brings a green dimension to urban living.

Right Gardens don't have to be limited to spring-summer colour. Plants such as autumn-flowering cyclamen provide an important splash of colour when everything else in the garden prepares itself for winter.

Below You may not have a cottage garden as such, but you can always try some planting schemes reminiscent of hazy days in the country.

And persuading a few friends to muck in can go a long way towards easing the burden – just promise them a few beers when the work's done!

The good thing is that planting and pottering in the garden almost demand that you relax. While certain tasks might be necessary, they needn't be boring. A lecturer once said of hoeing, 'It's peaceful, just helps me relax'. This is exactly what gardening is all about. The sense of achievement you get from helping something to grow has to be experienced. A mate of mine who likes gardening says it reminds him of bringing up his two year old: nurture, clean up, watch it grow. Very rewarding!

There's no doubt it requires courage to take that first step, especially when you don't know much about the subject. But we all have to start somewhere. I've heard friends protest sadly that plants always seem to die on them, as if there's a secret formula to getting them to grow which they'll never know. Take houseplants, for example. Ever killed one? I'd be surprised if you hadn't – everyone does. It's an initiation into the gardening world.

And there's so much information on gardening out there that you might wish you'd never asked. There are books, magazines, nurseries, the Internet, your mum and dad – let alone the gardener next door. All you need is a spadeful or two of courage. Let's face it, we're not talking about something potentially life-threatening: this is gardening, plants, getting a bit dirty. You just have to be bold and get stuck in. After all, you may not want to be a 'gardener', but I bet you want something more pleasing to the eye than the piece of real estate you currently look out on.

Your urban paradise
is waiting to happen
– so get stuck in!

THROW AWAY THE RULE BOOK

The great thing about gardening is that you don't need to be an expert. Contrary to the established view, many aspects of horticulture and gardening are really easy to pick up. For example, when it comes to plants, just remember WALNUTS – a handy acronym that stands for Water, Air, Light, Nutrients, Temperature and Soil (but more about that on page 97). When you buy a plant, read about its character in a plant directory – how much light it prefers, whether it benefits from regular feeds, if it needs extra watering in dry spells, and so on. Then make a WALNUTS list so you know how to look after it. With only this tiny bit of research you'll soon be growing it just like a pro!

Now I'm going to talk boring for a moment, but bear with me... SOIL. Brown stuff. Dirty, underfoot, b-o-r-i-n-g. There. I knew that would make you switch off. Don't you need a whole laboratory to analyse your soil and unlock the enormous mystery of this alien stuff? Magical as it is, getting the best out of your soil needn't be a mystery. There's no need to embark on an extended science project. The not-so-secret ingredient is well-rotted organic matter, and lots of it. Before you plant anything, dig into the soil as much organic matter as you can, and each year add more of the magic stuff to replenish stocks – your plants will love you for it. Just think about nature and you'll begin to understand. Leaves, stems, dead and decaying growth all fall to the ground and rot, and the resulting organic matter feeds the plant which dropped the leaves. And that's it! The circle goes on and on *ad infinitum*. So, if we add loads and loads of organic matter to the soil, then we're not only mimicking nature but maybe also giving her a helping hand. The result? Healthier plants. More flowers. Less disease.

Of course, gardening is not quite that simple and I guarantee you will make mistakes. But really, mistakes don't matter one bit. How you cope with them and what you learn from them is what matters. Mistakes don't mean failure. More often than not they will turn out to be happy accidents – things that work, but in a way you didn't expect and couldn't have planned for. Gardening is an organic process, evolving and changing before

ORGANIC MATTER

Organic matter is the Superman of the gardening world – unbeatable, invincible, infallible. It can be horse manure, chicken poo, spent hops (if you're lucky enough to live near a brewery), spent mushroom compost or simple garden compost, which you can get for free if you make it yourself (see pages 34–5). Soils and plants alike rejoice when a gardener mentions organic matter, especially in an urban garden where soil quality can be diabolical. With a new house, in particular, all that building work can leave the soil compacted and full of rubble.

Well-rotted organic matter in the soil helps plants to benefit from nutrients before the rain washes them away. It helps retain water, too – vital in a sandy soil where water drains away too quickly. It will also improve the structure of thick clay soils which are prone to drainage problems in the other direction – they hold onto water when you want them to let it go. Even with good soil, a supply of quality organic matter is a gold mine. If you have a garden, buy it by the barrowload and store it bagged up out of sight. If you have a balcony or a roof terrace, buy a couple of bags, and when you pot up any plants, mix it into your potting compost.

Right Organic matter is the starting point for all healthy plants. Spend a bit of time digging it into your garden, and those couple of hours labour will pay dividends in the months to come.

your eyes. Plants are living beings and, like stroppy teenagers, they don't always want to follow the rules. And sometimes that's just fine.

For example, one of my favourite plants is love-in-a-mist (or nigella, if you're posh), a lovely name for one of the prettiest annuals going. However, it's a prolific seeder, spreading itself all around a garden. I used to curse it, but soon gave up battling against the numerous seedlings. Wherever I looked, delicate blue flowers and gorgeous puffy balloon seedheads were popping up between all the other plants. I would never have imagined or planned this. Sometimes nature just does it better.

LATIN NAMES

How can you possibly be a successful gardener if you are not familiar with *Betula albosinensis* var. *septentrionalis* (simply a long, 'orrible name for a relative of the common silver birch)? Just remember that Latin nomenclature can be a power game played by horticultural big-heads in order to make you feel small. But Latin is a universal language, a kind of plant Esperanto, and botanical (Latin) names exist mainly for identification purposes and for plants where there's no common name. By using the Latin names, people in Japan can order plants in England knowing they'll get exactly what they ask for – even if they don't speak any English. But common names are just as good when you're starting out (except when ordering plants from Japan!). And, like it or not, you'll probably pick up Latin names anyway, without even realising it.

THE ART OF THE POSSIBLE

Many see gardening merely as a spectator sport, primarily due to the snobbery that surrounds the subject, and that's unfortunate. And what better place to illustrate this than the elitism attached to Latin names? Another cause of frustration is in not knowing what even common gardening terms mean – and thinking you ought to know. Terms like hardy annual, biennial, herbaceous perennial. Even my mum asked me for a definition of 'half-shade' last week, saying that the term has confused her for years. This book will endeavour to clarify those everyday horticultural terms which seem to get glossed over, just because it's assumed we should all know what they refer to.

Some of the techniques involved in gardening and garden design are difficult to pick up from books. Gardening is a learning process which involves time, practice and hands-on experience. You also need patience in bucketloads. So don't

Above The simplest designs work best, allowing shapes and materials to set the style, without cluttering up the garden space.

Above left The annual love-in-a-mist (*Nigella damascena*) will seed itself freely all over a garden, providing attractive seedheads to follow the lovely pale blue flowers.

A good rule of thumb is to keep gardening and garden design simple. Why over-complicate things? It's less hassle to keep things simple. Often the most effective garden designs can be achieved by choosing a few different plants that look good together, repeated around the garden in various combinations. A grandiose scheme will give you more problems than solutions, and lead to the waste of hard-earned cash into the bargain.

Even with this in mind, you'll probably find that arriving at a simple design is not as easy as you first thought. Everybody, especially those just starting out, can be guilty of being over-ambitious, partly because it's such fun to play about with plans and ideas. I used to be a classic case. I was always tempted to plant too close together to cover that bare earth, and then I'd have to move everything further apart the following year. Instant coffee, instant garden – I've been there. Just remember that it's easy to add to a simple design at a later date when the enthusiasm kicks in, but it can be very difficult to remove or re-design an elaborate feature without disrupting the whole garden. A simple design is also more eye-catching, especially in a small garden, balcony or roof terrace where space is at a premium.

GETTING BACK TO PLANTS

The world of gardening is going through a funny time at the moment, with an eclectic mix of styles and opinions. You could end up with some very expensive hard landscaping, or a folly which will annoy the neighbours and quickly go out of fashion, or you could go for a softer, more chilled approach. Contrary to much contemporary thinking, you don't always have to sweat with that concrete mixer. Personally I can't justify spending stacks of money on extravagant man-made features, especially those which use loads of ready-mix. I like to think the earth needs to breathe a bit, not wear a concrete cap. Plants can provide as much interest, enjoyment and excitement as any exorbitant bit of hard landscaping or designer fix.

Plants are exciting, believe me. Take the candyfloss tree (*Cercidiphyllum japonicum*) with its incredible scent of burnt sugar; the regal lily (*Lilium regale*), reminding you of a summer-afternoon boudoir; the startling red stems of the willows (*Salix*) and dogwoods (*Cornus*) in winter, when you think everything's gone to earth; the royal purple of foxgloves (*Digitalis*); the early *Crocus ancyrensis*, with masses of small yellow flowers the colour of egg-yolks in gloomiest January. Nature's on the move and the gardener's sap rises with her.

Above top Planning your planting scheme will help eliminate the potential for costly mistakes.
Above Some of the best planting schemes involve gorgeous grasses and architectural plants – you don't have to use summer annuals to create something impressive.

be dismayed when you first start out. You may have limited or even no knowledge when it comes to plants, but this can only get better the more you explore the subject and go for what grabs you in particular. You'll also read magazines and books on garden design and will be surprised by what new ideas you absorb. Yet you'll probably find you already possess the skills needed to design your own garden space, it's just a question of transferring these skills outdoors. You simply take what you practise inside your house and carry it outside. For example, when you re-design or decorate your home, you're using the very same selection process of choosing colour, placement of form and shape, and awareness of texture that you use when designing a garden. The only difference is that the materials are a little unfamiliar at first.

Left Tiny gardens can still be fantastically impressive. For this planting scheme, I used lots of evergreens such as *Choisya ternata* 'Sundance' and *Pittosporum tobira* 'Variegata' to create some all-year-round interest.

MY OWN ROOTS

My love of gardening, and especially of plants, was not formed overnight. I started in horticulture too young to fully appreciate the plant world. Like most teenage boys, my only interests were alcohol, girls and making music. Gardening was something my mum did, and was therefore something I didn't.

My first job in the horticulture industry was at a local smallholding which grew and sold most of its own produce, like carrots, potatoes, apples. I loved it. There was a small group of us who'd roam around the farm, sun or rain, picking sprouts, cutting broccoli and planting leeks at the direction of the owner. This experience then led me to various stints at colleges where my growing enthusiasm was fuelled by staff who were among the most fanatical horticulturists I have ever known. Yet I still hadn't found something which I think every real gardener needs – a passion. That changed when I was working at a nursery in Somerset and met up with the great love of my life: trees!

When I talk about trees I get a bit dewy-eyed. Trees are my passion. I can't get enough of them. I love their hulking size or their sublime delicacy, the colour of their autumn leaves that cloak the ground at their base with an orangey-gold shadow. I love the colour of their bark, too, which brings life to a garden when other plants have died back over winter. Trees always hold their own, no matter what the season, and there's a tree for every situation.

Want a tree for a pot on a roof terrace? Try the purple birch (*Betula pendula* 'Purpurea'). Want a tree that chucks out a drunken scent next to a

Left *Prunus* 'Taihaku' simply flowers and flowers through-out spring.
Above *Betula pendula* 'Youngii' is one of a few birches suitable for urban gardens because of its compact growth.

house? Try the evergreen *Magnolia grandiflora*. A tree to almost touch the sky (and suck out all the ground water roundabout)? Try the Lombardy poplar (*Populus nigra* var. *italica*). A tree to flower so profusely that the air is a mist of frothy petals? That's the great white cherry (*Prunus* 'Taihaku').

An arboretum (a Victorian collection of trees) is one of my favourite places. Just walking around gives you a sense of how small you are. There are trees in California which are over 3,000 years old –

Above It is possible to combine eating areas, privacy, lush planting and a sense of tranquility in a small, urban environment. Sculptures also have their place, but never underestimate the importance of plants!

awe inspiring! If there's one thing likely to catch my wandering attention span it's a tall, handsome tree in its prime. As well as being attractive, many trees are also exceptionally useful. They can give immediate backbone to a design, essential shade in a south-facing garden, an instant focal point, a superb wildlife habitat, or a screen for that ugly eyesore. And they are usually cheaper and less labour-intensive than any piece of hard landscaping.

I want to encourage you to use plants in your designs as much as possible. It's time to move away from the garden as fetish – with all kinds of weird and wonderful man-made and concrete structures – and put plants centre-stage again. I have so many favourites in the plant world that my head spins. Like every gardener, I also have my pet hates. I'm not too keen on summer bedding plants – all that work for something that only lives for about six months. My mum grows them in pots, though, and moves them around the garden to fill in gaps after a shrub has flowered, and it seems to work well. I'll introduce you to all my favourite plants in chapter 7 (and those I hate), but you'll get to know most of them as we go along.

Contrary to popular belief, plants are not there to bring you grief. Nor do they want to die on you. Plants are like people, they have their own specific

personalities – and they want to flourish. Like us, they have individual requirements which need to be understood. 'Give me acidic soil,' cries the Rhododendron. 'Give me a hard spring pruning so I can flower profusely in summer,' hollers the Buddleja. 'Gimme wet shade,' whimpers the Hosta.

And yes, it's true, there are some cussed plants which won't seem to grow anywhere, except in those coffee table books or in your neighbour's front garden. And these are always, but always, the ones I want to grow. However, there are also thousands of plants which aren't over-sensitive and which will tolerate a bit of serious neglect. A little knowledge about which plants to select and how to look after them is all you need.

The importance of plants to the urban dweller cannot be overestimated. Urban life is often full of stress, with all the pollution, congestion and noise. Plants can provide a source of inspiration and relief from our busy routines. After a bad day at work, imagine: returning home to a beautiful garden ...or chilling with a glass of wine on a verdant balcony ...or letting the perfume drift indoors from a window box overflowing with sweet-scented pansies. After a hard day's graft, our little piece of the urban jungle can soothe and relax us – giving us the fortitude to go out and do it all over again.

YOUR LITTLE PIECE OF URBAN SPACE

'But I haven't really got a garden!' cries the urban gardener. 'It's just a back yard – a place to keep the rubbish bins, somewhere to string up the clothes line.'

All too often, city gardeners see only the problems, get depressed, then throw up their hands in despair. Looking in gardening books and magazines merely seems to emphasise that no one has a garden space as difficult and unattractive as yours. No wonder many think gardening is for others – for those who have level, south-facing land, with no overhanging trees, no ugly eyesores. Then there's the myth that gardening proper happens only in the country. Rubbish!

Your little piece of urban space matters. Whether it's to the front or the back of your house, you look out on it most days, and you walk through it whenever you come and go. To some, the garden merely comes with the house and is not a priority – but city living decrees that we make the most of all we have. Your outdoor space is yours to decorate and furnish as you please – it becomes a reflection of you. Just as the interior of your home and the clothes you wear tell others about your tastes, about where you're coming from, so, too, does your garden. And even the darkest, smallest, grottiest, concrete-covered back yard has potential. It really does.

The secret is to work with the space you've got, not hanker for the garden next door. Working with what you have is a reality check. Trying to design a cottage garden for a 5 x 5m/16 x 16ft basement plot won't work. But if cottage gardens are your thing, you can always incorporate plants and smaller-scale structures which characterise the cottage garden proper, even if you can't manage the rose-covered walkway!

No urban garden space is too small, too ugly, too overlooked or too dark to be improved – transformed even. To get yourself motivated, just fantasise about how you'll feel when you have a gorgeous outdoor room to lounge in, cappuccino in hand, on a lazy Sunday morning. Feels good, doesn't it? From these pleasant imaginings, take the plunge, play with ideas in your mind, get fired up. Anything is possible if you have the motivation and willpower to carry it through.

Below Everybody dreams of having their own little portion of paradise, away from the crowds. Creating such a spot needn't be as difficult as you might think.

YOUR GARDEN IS IMPORTANT

If you live and work in an urban environment, the chances are that you don't have much time or energy to get out into the country and relax. When the weekend comes and you feel you must get away, think what generally happens: unless you leave your home at some godforsaken hour in the morning you'll find yourself in a line of traffic in the company of everyone else who's fleeing the city for a piece of rural bliss.

If you're an urbanite you don't need reminding that the only quick thing about travelling by car is the speed at which journeys are becoming a first-degree nightmare. The word 'travel' used to mean that you felt you were getting somewhere, enjoying the ride, watching the scenery. But now all that happens is you get very familiar with the exhaust of the car in front, and for hour upon hour the countryside remains as distant as ever. Journeying isn't the fun it was – and it eats into the few hours you manage to snatch under those dreamy scented lime trees by the river.

But there's a simple remedy: turn your garden space into an outdoor des res, and you won't feel so trapped by city living. You can give up on those coast-to-coast traffic jams and have a holiday on your back doorstep, sunbathing, cooling down by the pond, eating and drinking like kings (without the worries of drink-driving), watching the wildlife and having the whole day – or weekend – for relaxation. More important, your garden will be there for you all the time, looking beautiful, ready for you to enjoy those vital breaks, long or short, when you just want to collapse in a chair and empty your mind after work.

Below What could be more relaxing than spending Sunday morning chilling out in your urban hideaway? Weigh up the benefits of a calm outdoor space compared to the lemming-like traffic exodus on weekends and bank holidays.

Bottom left Clematis add a splash of colour and help to provide privacy from neighbours.

Bottom right Entertaining in the garden is a more relaxed, more informal experience – and you can party on till whatever time you like.

Below Clever screening will help to convert your garden into another room, complete with privacy and some sound resistance.

For those who work from home, it's all the more important to have a pleasant environment to wander into, especially in summer. And even in winter you can draw the eye outdoors by setting up strings of fairy lights to run through your trees – bringing a little bit of magic on a grey January day. For the home-based worker the garden is a therapeutic place in which to potter and tinker in all seasons, while your mind mulls over a work-related problem.

In what other ways is your urban space significant? If you have an urban lifestyle, your exposure to nature is probably limited. So using and optimising your garden is important – both for you and for the urban environment.

A 'LIVING' ROOM

In cramped cities, that unused piece of garden can also become an extension of your living space. Since city life is expensive and house prices so exorbitant, people often have less rooms than they would like. By redefining your garden space vertically and horizontally – with pergolas, trellis and planting, for example – you can transform your garden or balcony into another room or intimate space. Taking this even further, you could suspend canvas sails over seating areas to create a private space in an overlooked patio or courtyard; trail grape vines over the verandah to recreate that Mediterranean touch or drape bowers and arbours with scented roses and jasmines to transport yourself to the Middle East. If you're lucky enough to have a fairly large garden, you could even divide it off into a couple of rooms – each with a different 'feel' or for a different use – one for the kids, perhaps, and one for you. Yes, you might use this extra room for only half the year due to our climate. However, I'll bet that with a little imagination and forethought you'll get more out of your garden space than some of the rooms in your house.

'Eating out' also takes on a totally different connotation when you entertain friends in your garden. Suddenly it's far less expensive, far more relaxing, much more fun. You can take as long as you like over the meal, and there are no waiters hurrying you on in order to make way for the next set of punters. The food itself tastes so much better when eaten out of doors – and the time you would normally spend driving to and from the restaurant can be added to the leisure time enjoyed in the garden.

BACK TO NATURE

In an urban environment any green space is a sanctuary. And getting in touch with Mother Earth, through such activities as digging the soil and planting, is essential to our well-being. It sounds like a tired cliché, a leftover from hippydom, but we owe all that we are to Mother Earth, so we'd better look after her!

In an uncertain and insecure world there's a quiet revolution going on. More and more people are getting back to nature and spending time and effort making the space where they live meaningful and nurturing. The nesting instinct is taking over in the garden as a backlash against all that pointless consumerism. Your garden, however tiny, is part of our planet and is just as valuable and vital as any other part, large or small. Nature is as much alive and in evidence in your urban space as on a Welsh hillside – it's just a different slice of the pie.

When you plant a hosta, for example, you do have to look after it a little, by planting it in good quality soil and watering it when the ground is dry. But it actually does the growing all by itself – a little piece of nature at work in your back yard. All over the world seeds and cuttings get planted, watered, protected and watched over until the plant just takes off. You can feel real pride when you work in alignment with nature – and it just happens to be fun at the same time.

To get further in touch with Mother Earth, try growing your own produce. You can successfully grow edible crops in the smallest of spaces, even in pots, and most of these plants are decorative, too. The easiest and most productive food plants for the urban garden include tomatoes, runner beans, courgettes and herbs, all of which will grow well in tubs; herbs will even do well in window boxes or in pots on your windowsill.

The garden as therapy isn't a new concept, but it's becoming more popular as city dwellers try to make the most of the space they have, and turn it into a nurturing environment. It's important to work with what you have. If you have a shady garden, then don't go for plants which require sunny conditions, instead capitalise on shade-lovers like ivies, ferns, camellias, bergenias and hostas. Lush foliage in different greens and leaf shapes creates the feeling of a grotto or sanctuary. And if you have an area which catches the sun, there you can grow tubs of flowering plants ready to bring into the shady space when they are in full bloom (flowers often last longer in cooler, shadier spots than in the full heat of the sun).

GREENING THE CITY

To many, the city is a concrete jungle, its very nature identified by its buildings and structures. But it needn't be like this. Going green is a way of redressing the balance, by which I mean putting plants centre-stage – my key phrase throughout this book.

There is a school of thought that says we should mimic our surroundings when we design spaces for outdoor living. If we're surrounded by

Above Combining both colour and a wonderful scent, catmint (Nepeta) is a hard-working plant – just watch out for the local moggies!

Far right Arbours smothered in climbers are ideal for adding height and concealing ugly views.

Right Many 'exotic' plants, such as the chusan palm (*Trachycarpus fortunei*), will survive in the protected environment of a city garden.

brick or concrete, so the theory goes, we should use it liberally in the garden to provide some kind of continuity, a sympathy with the environment around us. If you imagine the kind of environment we might have if we always adhered to this principle, we would have a very grim city indeed! This is why I am trying to encourage gardeners to go for more naturalistic materials like wood and stone. And plants, of course – don't forget the star performers!

Plants can fulfil almost all of our 'architectural' needs. We need to look more closely at their shape to see how they can be used in this respect, and not, as most of us do, go straight for the flowers. Using plants as design features in their own right isn't new, but all too often plants are seen as an adjunct, a bit of softening around the edges, while you hire a concrete mixer and hard-landscape your garden. When I look at a garden my first thought is 'What plants can I incorporate here?', not 'What paving can I use?' Remember that hard landscaping should serve the beauty of the plants, not vice versa.

Take the garden path, for instance. Rather than a load of ready-mix, why not use gravel or chipped bark? Bark especially gives a more sympathetic path, which works particularly well if you lay it over a porous membrane to stop the odd weed coming through. I'm developing quite a fondness for the stuff. It looks really stylish, smells nice, especially after rain, is soft underfoot, and it gives a bit back to the soil beneath as it gently decomposes. Bark provides cover for invertebrates, too – just watch blackbirds flicking it aside first thing in the morning! And for those of you on a tight budget, it's cheap, cheap, cheap. And it doesn't detract from the plants one bit.

Rather than simply raising the height of a boundary wall or fence, trees can be used to give privacy and block out ugly views. And why not grow a hedge rather than build a fence? Try sculptures made from living willow as your focal points, create arbours and pergolas to show off beautiful climbers. Make 'greening the city' your buzzwords for the new millennium.

A GARDEN FOR ALL SEASONS

Gardens often have the misfortune to be considered in terms of summer alone. This is a pity. City dwellers can follow the seasons and stay in touch with nature just as much as those who live in the country – in fact, it's essential to make your garden work hard for its keep all year long. For strong, structural elements to give what gardeners refer to as 'backbone', you need to choose plants that don't just flower in summer and then disappear in winter, leaving you nothing but bare earth to look at. Go for at least some planting which gives interest all year round: plants which are evergreen or have winter form, which also flower, then produce berries, and perhaps are also richly perfumed.

Some of my favourite, most garden-worthy plants for both summer and winter include:
- barberry (*Berberis*) and firethorn (*Pyracantha*), both evergreen shrubs with both flowers and bright autumn berries
- *Rosa rugosa*, with flowers, scent, healthy foliage and large red hips in winter
- *Rosa sempervirens*, with its late summer flowers, and light semi-evergreen foliage
- evergreen Christmas box (*Sarcococca*) with intense winter perfume and suitable for even dense shade
- Camellias, with showy spring flowers and shiny evergreen foliage
- *Trachelospermum jasminoides*, an evergreen climber with small glossy leaves and jasmine-like scented flowers, which thrives in semi-shade

THE DIFFICULTIES OF CITY GARDENING

We've looked at the benefits of improving your garden space. But what about all the problems that city gardens seem to attract? Well, there are problems specific to the urban environment, and it's worth facing these head on. You have to identify a problem before you can deal with it, of course, so see if you recognise any of the following common drawbacks.

ACCESS

Common to many urban gardens is the lack of separate rear access, which means you will have to carry all your gardening supplies through the house. This is something to consider when you think about what you'd like in your garden. Soil, compost, paving materials might all need to be barrowed through your hallway, so check that doorways are wide enough, and be sure to protect the flooring en route. And if you decide you need a mature specimen of a plant, before buying think about whether you will be able to manoeuvre it safely through the house.

AIR POLLUTION

Airborne pollution – from traffic, in particular – is ever present in the city. It is less noticeable when the weather is windy, but on a gorgeous sunny day, the overstuffed smell of exhaust fumes settles down in the atmosphere, making the air feel all used up. 'Inversion' is the weatherman's term for this particular hell in the city.

We don't enjoy suffocating in polluted air, and – surprise, surprise – most plants aren't too keen on it, either. But don't despair – there are some plants which don't mind pollution in the least. The London

Far left A year-round garden can be achieved with only a minimum of plants. Try some winter violas if you like cheerful colours on grey days.
Left Night-scented stocks (*Matthiola bicornis*) are excellent for counteracting the smell of urban smog.

plane tree is an example of a tree often chosen for its ability to withstand airborne clag, which is why it is found in so many streets, squares and city parks. You would not choose to plant this particular tree in your urban garden, as it's rather large, but when you visit a nursery, ask if the plants you fancy will grow in a city atmosphere. This will ensure that you don't choose some delicate exotic which protests and sulks when you get it home.

Make full use of scented plants to disguise the fumes; choose especially from those which are free with their scent, like night-scented stocks, so that your garden fills up with delicious perfumes that help to cancel out the bad odours – a bit like the principle of an air freshener in a smelly room. Fill the garden with fragrant plants that flower in summer, because that's when you'll use your garden most, but remember to place some wonderful winter-scented plants near a doorway, so you can appreciate them as you go in or out of the house.

mind then edits out the undesirable noise, or at least finds it bearable. Wind chimes also catch the attention, both the tiny tinkly ones and the larger ones made of bamboo. Attracting birds into the garden is also a good idea; they're fun to watch and sing their hearts out in spring. And with a dovecote or even a bird table in the garden you'll think you are in the middle of a rural idyll – and so will your neighbours. And again, you can use plants to help muffle intrusive urban noises: those that rustle, like bamboos and other tall grasses, are invaluable to the urban gardener. There is nothing quite like a clump of tall miscanthus wafting in the wind to mask the constant hum of a local busy road – as well as giving your urban space a peaceful, relaxing air.

Above A small barrel pond with a fountain is a compact water feature for an urban garden, and the gentle splash of water will help to drown out noise pollution.

Above right Growing plants in pots and raised beds is a good solution where the soil is poor or even polluted. A two-tier pond has also been created in containers.

NOISE POLLUTION

This is another pollutant that is difficult to escape from. In fact, of all the common pollutants, noise is probably the most stressful for urban dwellers. Traffic is all around you – you can't do anything about that – but noisy and inconsiderate neighbours can make your outdoor life a misery (don't become one yourself!). For the odd party, playing music outdoors is fine, but loud music and radios blaring away in the garden are serious bad news, and add to the overall noise levels outdoors.

To deal with noise pollution you have to be cunning. Try to incorporate something into your garden design which focuses the ear on a pleasing sound within your own outdoor space, such as a fountain in a pond, or a splashing waterfall. The

POLLUTED SOIL

This is not a common problem, but you may be unlucky enough to have soil in which nothing will grow successfully. The gardens of houses built on 'brownfield' sites may have clinker or ash disguised by merely the thinnest covering of topsoil, and gardens on new estates sometimes have builder's rubble hidden under a skim of grass. The obvious answer to these problems is to get rid of as much of the rubble as you can (contractor's job) and bring in new topsoil. However, if you have a heavily polluted soil and can't face the hassle and expense of replacing it all, why not grow all your plants in containers or raised beds? This way you can dictate the quality of the soil, and it will save a lot of bending – and possible back pain.

WILDLIFE IN THE CITY

Garden wildlife appreciates the urban microclimate as much as plants do. It's not necessary to have a wilderness to have wildlife – you don't need to have a messy garden in order to attract wild creatures. You can have a peaceful haven for yourself that's easy to look after, and enjoy wild birds and animals at the same time. If you make your garden attractive to them, you may be lucky enough to attract hedgehogs and slow-worms – both voracious slug-munchers!

The presence of wildlife in your garden demonstrates good energy, positive chi – one of the principles of good Feng Shui. And you will benefit from the movement, sound, colour, life and the excitement of seeing nature come to you. So what can you do to attract wildlife? First of all, try not to use chemicals in your garden, since they destroy the all-important food chain. Think organic wherever possible. Nature will balance out the pests with their natural predators, as long as you don't interfere too much.

Most wildlife loves water. A pond in some form or another is a must (if you have very young children, cover it securely with a strong metal grille to prevent accidents). For very small gardens or terraces, a half-barrel will do just fine. Toads, frogs and even newts (which seem to appear from nowhere by magic!) will quickly colonise your pond, as will the formidable-looking larvae of dragonflies and damselflies. And on warm summer evenings you will be serenaded by your very own frog choir! Be sure to include a shallow end and a gentle gradient down into the water, so creatures can easily get in and out of the pond. In this shallow area, position a few flat rocks or pebbles, half in, half out of the water. Then insects like honey bees won't drown when they come to have a drink.

Native trees and shrubs are best for wildlife because our indigenous fauna has evolved to feed off these species, not on something which originates in, say, Australia. The silver birch (*Betula pendula*), ideal for urban gardens, supports over 200 species of insects, which in turn are eaten by birds and other predators. And native often means cheaper and no worrying over the growing requirements of 'exotics'.

Our native birds are on the decline and urban gardeners can play a vital role in keeping bird populations buoyant. All you need to do is put up feeders and bird tables, then fill them with nuts and seeds. Hulled sunflower seeds and peanuts are both excellent bird foods, don't leave a mess, don't cost a fortune, and are easy to use in hanging feeders. Bulk buying nuts and seeds from pet shops makes them even cheaper. If you have a problem with squirrels eating all the nuts you put out for the birds, buy special squirrel-proof feeders, and then laugh at their futile antics! Do put out food all year round; it's a myth that birds only need feeding in winter. You can also put up nest boxes – blue tits and robins will be your most likely takers. As a reward to feeding them, blue tits will eat the greenfly on your roses, while thrushes will go for the slugs and snails.

Berrying shrubs will invite blackbirds and fieldfares to visit your garden. Birds do have favourite berries and they can strip a shrub bare if they've found the lunch they prefer – so be prepared to share your garden's autumn bounty. Rowan (*Sorbus*) and cotoneaster seem to be *haute cuisine* in this respect.

To attract bees and butterflies plant the nectar-rich ice plant (*Sedum spectabile*), lavender (*Lavandula*), globe thistle (*Echinops*) and old-fashioned blue-flowered plants in general. Buddleja is another favourite; in summer this is an absolute magnet for butterflies – I once counted 30 on one bush alone. Encouraging bees is important as they are the number one pollinator, which makes them a vital part of the ecosystem and an asset to your flowers, fruits and vegetables. Bees forage early, so plant lots of crocuses for early food supplies, and if you have ivy growing let it flower in autumn, as the bees will appreciate that too. Always try to leave some areas undisturbed, looking a little 'wild', so that you'll attract invertebrates which feed other creatures in the wildlife food chain.

There are a few caveats to do with feeding wildlife: don't put out cooked food, or you are likely to encourage rats, and don't scatter grain unless you want to attract all the city's pigeons.

SHRUBS TO ATTRACT BUTTERFLIES

- *Lavandula stoechas* (French lavender)
- *Lavandula angustifolia* 'Hidcote' (lavender)
- *Rubus cockburnianus*
- *Salvia officinalis* (sage)
- *Escallonia* 'Apple Blossom'
- *Thymus vulgaris* (common thyme)

SMALL TREES TO ATTRACT BIRDS

- *Sorbus cashmiriana* (Kashmir rowan)
- *Sorbus* 'Joseph Rock' (rowan)
- *Malus* 'Golden Hornet' (crab apple)
- *Malus* 'John Downie' (crab apple)
- *Crataegus laevigata* 'Paul's Scarlet' (hawthorn)
- *Ilex x altaclerensis* 'Golden King' (holly)

SMALL TREES TO ENCOURAGE BEES

- *Cercis siliquastrum* (Judas tree)
- *Caragana arborescens* (pea tree)
- *Prunus* spp. (cherry)
- *Malus* spp. (apple)
- *Mespilus germanica* (medlar)
- *Laurus nobilis* (sweet bay)

1: *Lavandula stoechas* (French lavender)
2: *Sorbus cashmiriana* (Kashmir rowan)
3: *Cercis siliquastrum* (Judas tree)
4: Bee on scabious (*Scabiosa*)
5: Painted Lady butterfly on a dahlia
6: Blue tit feeding
7: A frog

OVERCROWDED AND OVERLOOKED

In an urban situation you're lucky if you're not overlooked by other buildings – from the sides, from above, and sometimes even from below. Shrubs and trees are very successful in creating a screen, acting as a buffer to the world outside and allowing you to pretend your neighbours are not there. If you sit in the middle of your tiny urban space, surrounded by vibrant green, what the eye cannot see should not trouble you too much.

One of the best urban spaces I know is a tiny shaded area at the back of a terraced house in the middle of some of the densest housing in London. The area is about the size of an average town patio, surrounded by very high walling on one side, and fencing on the other. Luckily, the gardens which back onto it contain some mature trees, and those on either side are filled with mature shrubs. You might think that a garden barely eight metres square with rows of densely packed houses all around would make for a hemmed-in claustrophobic feeling. But the effect is quite different. The owner has planted climbers which like shade – climbing hydrangea, ivy and golden hop – all around her tiny outdoor room, cloaking every surface with green. The green blends in with the trees behind and to either side, making her garden seem much bigger than it really is. She has neatly 'borrowed' the view of trees and shrubs beyond her garden, and made them part of her own outlook. And when you step out into her garden the effect is one of cool tranquillity, a real chill-out zone. A large barrel pond with a fountain contributes to the inward-looking mood created by the lush green planting and I noticed, too, a hot-tub tucked away between the ferns. Cool!

The restricted space available for plants in city gardens could be seen as a problem. A small courtyard just won't do justice to a massed planting as well as providing adequate space for bins, clothes lines, water features and potting shed. So make sure you scale down your ideas to fit the space available, and try always to leave ample room for access to your plants so that they can be tended, pruned and watered as necessary.

EYESORES

Take a critical look at your garden from inside the house, then move outdoors and list all the horrible features within sight. You may have an electricity sub-station or a pylon close by, or a railway line running past the bottom of your garden, close enough for all the passengers to look straight in every time a train goes past. Or your 'view' might be a featureless grey concrete wall some 10m/33ft high, a tower block looming all too near, or even your neighbour's hideous home-made shed!

There are very few eyesores which can't be alleviated by some clever planting. The key words here are 'screening' and 'disguise', and a little judicious placing of your favourite plants can work wonders. Climbers can ramble over old sheds, and trellis and vertical planting can screen off those areas where you keep dustbins, compost bins, and the ubiquitous rotary clothes dryer. Eyesores within the garden which prove just too difficult to demolish or remove can be hidden by trees or shrubs. And for large, immovable problems like tower blocks, pylons or factories, adopt a two-pronged approach: screen what you can with trees, then try to draw the eye away from the boundaries and into the garden by creating focal points and eye-catching colour combinations.

REFUSE AND RUBBISH

Most of us live in situations which are far from ideal, but we have to learn to make the best of what we have. How many urban gardens do you know which are nothing more than resting places for rubbish sacks and wheelie bins? How many back yards littered with bits of old cars and motorbikes, or piles of rotting wood – rubbish that the owner always meant to take to the local tip but somehow never got round to dealing with? Most people find dealing with clutter in their houses daunting enough, without having to consider the garden as well.

But all gardens benefit from a concerted clean-up, and on a day when you feel like chucking out

Below left If you have rear or side access, this will make it much easier to transport plants and materials into the garden – and to give it a good clear-up when needed.
Below Drains and pipes – as well as sheds and fences – can all be partially concealed with verdant climbers.

Right Storage is always a problem for gardeners, but you can help to conceal ugly sheds with some carefully positioned plants and bushes.

Below The hard fern, (*Blechnum spicant*) enjoys a shady environment and so adds some interesting shapes to difficult gardens that see very little sunlight.

the junk in your house, extend your enthusiasm to the garden. Throwing out all those broken plastic pots you'll never use, but which you stacked beside the shed 'just in case', is an excellent way to start. Dead plants are eyesores, too, and need to be dug up and disposed of. Clean up the whole garden space, including the edges and corners where slugs and snails love to congregate. You want your eye to be drawn by beauty, not ugliness, and in the city we need to make a point of creating attractive spaces wherever we can.

WIND

It's not only coastal areas which suffer from excess wind. Densely built-up areas can also have their fair share. Some wind problems are specific to the urban environment – tall buildings give rise to local gusting, and the creation of wind tunnels. Solid obstacles like walls or fences are not the best solution to blocking the wind: they just cause it to come roaring over with a vengeance. Instead you need to filter and slow the wind down, using permeable obstacles such as hedges, trees, trelliswork and board-on-board fencing.

Balconies and roof terraces often have serious problems with over-exposure to the elements. Here you'll need screening, as well as plants that tolerate desiccation by sun and wind – and maybe even a simple automatic irrigation system to ensure they don't dry out. Good plants include bamboos, grasses and glossy-leaved evergreens like aucuba, pittosporum and escallonia, with 'choicer' plants interspaced in the shelter of wind-resistant shrubs.

SHADE

Dense shade is a feature of many urban gardens which are surrounded by high fencing or walling on all sides. You, or your neighbour, might have an attractive tree or two, but they will probably cast deep shade over the rest of your garden. You may have a north-facing garden which only sees the sun for a few months of the year. But shade isn't the problem you might have been led to believe. A lot of plants relish it. True, most flowering plants do need some sun, but even a garden which sees no direct sunlight can become a green oasis, with an atmosphere like no other. And you can introduce temporary tubs of flowering plants to enliven shady spots with vibrant colour in summer.

There are other tricks to deploy. Light-coloured paints will brighten difficult areas and you can be creative with mirrors to reflect light into dark corners. Generally speaking, areas of dense shade are small, allowing you to concentrate your care and attention on them, to create something magical.

THE POSITIVE SIDE OF CITY GARDENING

Cities create a microclimate that's warmer and more protected than the surrounding countryside. And while they can be eyesores, many buildings actually protect your garden from the wind, as well absorbing heat throughout the day and releasing it at night – rather like a large storage heater. So make the most of this and give tender plants and exotics a try. How about a banana plant for that wow! factor, or brugmansias, with their huge, heavenly scented flowers, to knock your socks off? With a bit of luck and perseverance, your garden will be the envy of your country cousins.

Urban gardens tend to be much smaller than those in the country, but smaller also means more contained, and more easily managed, allowing for more care and attention per square metre for the same outlay. Small gardens have the exciting potential to be transformed into perfect, jewel-like stage sets, complete with unusual features such as *trompe l'oeil*, mirrored surfaces, sculptures and really special specimen plants, such as large bonsai, Japanese maples (*Acer palmatum* varieties) and tender exotics.

City gardens tend to be hemmed in by boundaries but if you have a boundary wall made of brick or stone, you are lucky. These natural materials make a wonderful backdrop for plants and you can go to town on vertical planting. You can also install a wall-mounted water feature, such as a spout with a small basin below.

In a small garden your money goes further since it's not being spread thinly over a large area, which means you have more to spend on enjoying yourself within it. There is good reason to make everything in your small garden really count.

WHERE
TO START

By now I expect your head's buzzing with ideas. Maybe, even, you're fired up and ready to transform your little piece of the urban jungle. Perhaps you've seen the results of other people's hard graft. But where do you start? What do you tackle first? The worst thing you could do is rush out to your nearest garden centre and load up the trolley with lots of impulse buys, then work out where on earth you're going to plant them all when you get home. Apart from anything, this is a sure-fire way of wasting money, and you wouldn't do the same thing if you were re-designing a room in your house, now would you? This chapter is designed to help you make that first move, starting with the basics. It's based on the way I approach designing a city garden in my professional life and gives little pointers to show how you can make the whole process as painless as possible.

Your first decision must be how much money you are willing to spend on your project. Decide on this, then write it large in your garden-planning notebook! You would of course need to do some initial preparation. It might sound obvious, but your research will help you to build a picture of what you're after. Flick through a few different gardening books – not just this one. At first it may seem like a confusing minefield, but you'll be surprised at just how much you absorb.

to have their say. The great thing about consulting your family and friends is that it whets their appetite. With luck they'll want to muck in and lend a hand, easing the burden on your shoulders and making the whole process more fun.

PEOPLE OR PRIVATE?

Decide whether you want the garden as a social space, primarily for entertaining. This often comes high on the list for urbanites. The idea of your

Below It's possible to create a quiet retreat while having a generous hard-surfaced area for entertaining.

EVALUATE WHAT YOU WANT AND NEED

What do you want your garden, balcony or roof terrace to be? And what does it need to do? What functions must it perform? That sounds obvious, but we seldom think about our outdoor spaces in these terms. It is a good idea to gather together your family, flatmates (and neighbours, if it's a communal garden), and ask them this question. In your notebook jot down what people say. Many of the responses you get will surprise everybody. Where are you going to store the refuse bins? How does Joe get to his bike? Small urban spaces need to be multifunctional, and satisfy the whole household. When the family sees the potential for creating a smashing outdoor room they'll all want

mates coming over and having dinner outside is often what appeals most when people get together and talk about transforming the garden. And for good reason: there's nothing like chilling outside with a beer in the evening sunshine. It's what gardens, urban or otherwise, are made for! On the other hand, you might want a place where you can collapse and chill out in your personal sanctuary. We all need somewhere to stretch out and relax, well away from other people and work, just to re-charge our batteries. What better use for your garden? It's right on your doorstep, with drink and eats but a minute away. You can, of course, mix the two functions, having a private corner for yourself, along with specially designed areas for socialising and entertaining. If you're an evening lounge lizard, you'll want some exterior lights and possibly an outdoor heater, so jot those down too.

If your space is minute or you have no time, your garden might be a no-go area in autumn and winter when it basically becomes what I call a 'picture' – something pretty to look out on from inside the house. Here, your design will need to look good all year round. Definite formal structures with a lot of evergreens will work best; colour can be introduced in pots of flowering plants according to the season. Fragrance may not get a look in because you're not outside to enjoy it!

FINDING THAT SUN-TRAP

If you want to sit in the sun, you'll need to identify where the sun shines at different times of the day. Think about when you're most likely to use your space: evenings, daytime, or weekends? If it's when you get home from work, you'll already know where to plonk your chair, so that's a good area to use for topping up your tan or socialising. It's no good surveying your plot from the back door, and marking out on paper the place for a sun terrace if you haven't checked where the sun shines when you want to be in the garden! That lovely spot which catches the morning sun might turn out to be dark and dingy come late afternoon. And, of course, the sun's position changes as the year moves on. It is a good idea to have a bench or two in different places round the garden, then you can catch the sun at all times of year and still plan your main space with the summer sun in mind.

CHILDREN IN THE GARDEN

Having young children will dramatically affect how you look at your space. Can you devote an area to a climbing frame, or somewhere the kids can kick a ball around? Will this conflict with the area you've set aside for supping wine? No-one needs reminding that kids get themselves into all sorts of trouble, so you'll need to keep your space as safe as possible – no structures with sharp edges, no

spiny, thorny or poisonous plants. One thing worth remembering when you're working out what you want from the garden is that children love to grow things, especially plants with a big Wow! factor, like sweet peas and giant sunflowers. Why not set aside a little patch where kids can experiment and grow simple plants? You'll find it very rewarding, as will they. My parents used to let my brother and me have a little piece of their garden – perhaps that's where my love of plants originated. Who knows?!

PLANTS VS. PEOPLE

If you've got the makings of a plant lover, or you're already a fanatic, make sure you devote enough space for your passion. I find there's nothing more

Above Wherever the sun falls in your garden, ensure you plan for a seat so you can stock up on some rays!

Above Growing your own food can be very rewarding, but work out the amount of space the plants take up before deciding to incorporate a vegetable plot.

THE NATIONAL GARDENS SCHEME
The gardens of the National Gardens Scheme are a great source of ideas and practical information, and you should try to visit any in your area. Made up of ordinary people who open their gardens to the public for charity, the scheme has been going for 75 years. There are loads of members in towns and cities throughout the country, some of which will be close to where you live, and have gardens with similar localised problems to your own. These gardeners will be used to the particular topography and climatic conditions associated with the locality. They will be able to offer advice, suggest suitable plants, recommend local suppliers and help with any other questions you have. To find the gardens nearest you, ask for the 'yellow book' at your local nursery or garden centre.

frustrating than not being able to grow all the plants I want on my balcony. I've got my bikes, a table and chairs and the washing line to contend with! Unfortunately my plants hardly get a look in – they just go where they can. It doesn't help that my girlfriend vetoes many of them – my lilies for example. 'Yes, I know the pollen may stain your clothing, but what about the glorious colour and the fabulous fragrance?' (She could just snip those stamens off!) It's a constant battle between what I want from my outside space and what we actually need it for. I guarantee that if plants are your passion you'll feel similarly thwarted. If you're lucky enough to have a big garden and don't devote sufficient space to the plants, you might just kick yourself.

KITCHEN GARDEN
Having your own kitchen-garden space in the city is a great idea for those who want to supplement supermarket food with their own. It used to be said that growing things to eat in the city was not good news because of the high concentration of lead in the air, but these days lead-free petrol is the norm. However, you might still think twice about feeding your family from veggies grown right along the busiest main road in your city.

The good news is that most gardens are fine for growing veg. But you have another problem to deal with: where to put your vegetable plot. Believe me, this can cause so many arguments. But if one of you wants to grow food, and the other flowers, you can compromise by growing them together in the French potager system, which combines both flowers and produce in a very formal design. And there's nothing to stop you growing veg, especially the more ornamental-looking types such as ruby chard and frilly-leaved lettuces, in among the flower beds. If you have a die-hard veggie-patch man (it's usually the men!) you'll be fighting over who has the best ground. Simply put, food needs the best soil and the most sun, and that's what will win out!

If you have both maximum sun and good soil, it's handy to site such a plot near the back door. That way you can tend your produce, keep a daily eye out for pests, and be able to pick something quickly if it's raining. If you can't see your plot from the door you may find yourself with an 'out of sight, out of mind' attitude, and neglect it. With a plot so near to the house, the challenge is to make it look fantastic. The main difficulty is that the plants are never in the ground for very long – sooner or later you're going to eat them! So the plot continually loses the very thing which gives it some structure. That's why you need to edge the area with bricks, boards, miniature hurdles or – as is traditional – by planting low hedges of box (*Buxus*).

BACK TO THE POTAGER

Most people's idea of a foodie patch in the garden is of a rectangle with wonky canes and bits of old net draped over makeshift structures, large spaces of bare earth, and veg grown in rows... not very creative and certainly not beautiful. This typical layout, which hasn't changed much for decades, is practical because it allows you to get between the rows to tend plants, but it seldom looks inspiring. If you have a big urban garden, you have the luxury of having a separate veggie area – but why does veg always have to be seen as something to hide?

In the potager, beauty and productiveness combine to give you a garden that's visually pleasing and, in most small urban spaces, that's exactly what you want. A potager is the French term for 'kitchen garden', where vegetables are grown alongside flowers, fruit and herbs. Vegetable varieties are selected carefully for their colour and form and used to make patterns in box-edged beds. As soon as one crop is pulled and eaten, another goes in to take its place.

HERBS ON HAND

Grow your herbs in a sunny spot near the back door if you can. You'll only need a small quantity for a meal, and if you plant herbs at the far end of the garden, you'll be loathe to run up there for a sprig of rosemary on a winter's day. Herbs take to pot culture well, and look attractive in their own right clustered together near where you can use them.

You can maximise your herb growing on a balcony or terrace, or even a window box. As well as looking great, herbs grown neatly in containers close to hand give you year-round attractiveness if they're evergreen, so try and grow them, even if you don't have the space for much else. Nothing impresses so much as using your own freshly picked herbs in cooking or as a garnish, and simply opening a window to stretch out and nip off a handful of sage or mint, shows real dedication!

ROOM FOR COMPOST

Not all of the kitchen garden is about beautifying, however. If you're really keen, sooner or later you'll want to make your own compost, and the eternal question will arise: where to put the compost heap?

You've seen allotment compost heaps and shuddered: old corrugated iron or rotting planks around a heap of smelly, decomposing vegetation. Ugh! But compost heaps don't have to be hideous. Although the process going on inside the bin is a bit on the ugly side, you don't need to see it. And to the plants, compost is the equivalent of having a triple fresh orange juice and a pile of vitamin-rich foods every day!

Compost isn't the stuff you buy in huge bags from the garden centre. The home-made sort is made with your own tender hands by saving those household scraps you usually put in the wheelie bin! We want to reduce the amount of land-fill rubbish, so putting your peelings and fruit skins out for refuse collection is not the best idea, anyway. Instead, save them for compost – they might not look much, but when rotted down they make the best plant food available – and all for free!

Above Turn your compost occasionally with a garden fork to let air into the mix and to amalgamate the layers.

IMPROVING THE LOOK OF YOUR COMPOST HEAP

Buying a purpose-built container makes a compost heap look tidier. Or you can make your own from slatted wood, and that'll be much more aesthetic! Compost bins are sold in garden centres and DIY stores. Most look like huge dustbins with the bottom cut off, although there are also bins on swivel stands or designs made of insulated material. You can place these in an out of the way place in the garden, even screen them off with trellis if you like. I've seen bins made from wood in the shape of beehives and these integrated well into the flower garden. Nobody knew exactly what they were, but they kept away thinking they'd get stung!

How do I get this marvellous composty stuff? Simple. All spent greenery, including garden waste, as well as shredded paper, eggshells, egg boxes and rotten fruit and veg can go into your compost. But don't put in cooked food, meat, or dog poo.

Compost-making is a doddle. You layer up all your kitchen waste and garden plant material much as you make a Black Forest gateau. Not too wet, not too dry. The aim is to have a pile of moist vegetation which will then rot down with minimal smell. You might have a layer of vegetable peelings, weeds (not the thick roots of perennials, though – those go in the wheelie), grass clippings, more weeds, a sprinkle of chicken manure pellets, a layer of kitchen waste, and so on until the bin's full. Then leave it while nature does all the work for you!

Back to the list you're making. Sulking apart, you have to identify what you need the garden for. It's vital to fit these components into your plan right at the beginning, otherwise you may end up with a fabulous garden but with a pile of bins, bikes, odds and sods in one corner and nowhere to put them! Rather ruins the effect, doesn't it?

STORAGE AND ACCESS

Storage is vital. Have you got bikes, and nowhere to store them? Are your rubbish bins kept in the garden? How can you fit them in with easy access, yet at the same time hide them? Garden tools, too, will need to be locked away from potential thieves. A shed will take the lot, but sheds are big things and tend to become horrible focal points. They need careful siting. If you can't fit one in, and there's no storage space inside the house, you'll need to come up with an ingenious storage method – perhaps a metal trunk that doubles as a seat, or a storage area hidden by trellis. If you don't have masses of room for storage, think about the things you could actually do without. But don't throw vital tools away: it's pointless having a lawn if you've no room for a lawn mower!

And what about the washing line? Folded-down rotary driers are not aesthetic! You need to remove them totally when not in use, yet store them for easy access too. That way you can still dry clothes in the sunniest part of the garden, but whip the pole out of the ground when the washing's dried and you want to sit there. It's that battle again – between what you want and what you need.

Do you have decent access to your garden, balcony or roof terrace? If not, do you need to construct a stairwell, some steps or a ramp? This should take priority in your budgeting. It's pointless spending money on a garden you can't get into!

Part of the preparation process is to survey your site. If this sounds like you need to be an engineer, or swan about with a theodolite, that's not what I mean! You don't need to do a scale plan or anything complicated. You should just measure up your space, and jot down the measurements on paper. It may not be the size you thought it was – inexplicably, it never is! Then look closely at your space under the following headings.

BOUNDARIES AND THE HARD BITS

The hard bits – fences, walls, paths and patios – make up what I call the skeleton of the garden. Basically, they hold your design together. They also have an enormous bearing upon the style, or 'feel', of your garden. So look closely at their condition. Can you keep what you've got? Or does any of it need to be moved or replaced? Think carefully and weigh up the replacement costs against aesthetic value. A dilapidated path, for example, will detract from even the most beautiful border: it'll make you notice what's wrong, rather than what's right, and will have to be replaced, whereas a shabby looking but sturdy fence can simply be renovated.

Cast an eye over the state of your boundary fences and walls. Does anything need fixing or replacing? If they're all right, keep them, even if they look slightly old-fashioned. Yes, there may be more stylish fences out there, such as reed and willow screens. But removing a sound boundary fence or wall, just for aesthetic reasons, will bump up the cost of your overall plan. You can always cover it with vigorous climbing plants, such as clematis, or give it a coat of paint, creating a completely new look.

If your boundary isn't solid, try to think further than ugly railings or chicken wire. You could plant a tall spiky hedge, like holly or hawthorn. Both will deter intruders, yet also encourage wildlife and provide a great backdrop to planting. You will have to trim those hedges, of course, but they'll look better than a prison camp!

If you already have a shed, leave it well alone, unless it's decrepit and falling apart – or in the wrong place entirely. Moving it is a hassle but it's possible, especially if it's plonked right in the middle of the garden's sunniest spot, just where you envisage sitting out. An old shed can easily be renovated, painted, and/or disguised with climbers and ramblers. Some old sheds look extremely characterful in their own right.

Above Grab a few tools and evaluate your space – it'll save time and money. **Left** Save and recycle bits and pieces you already have, if you think they'll come in handy. Odd bricks are always useful – and hanging on to them means one less load for the tip!

DRAINS, VENTS AND DPC

Here's where you get to play pretend-surveyor again. Identify the position and condition of drains, manhole covers and vents. You must keep access to these clear. Similarly, gas vents from central heating boilers and balanced-flue heaters need to be noted, so you don't block them off or build too close to them.

The height and position of the damp-proof course in your house walls will affect the construction of paved areas and raised beds. To find it, look at the bottom of the house walls. It will be recognisable by a course of different coloured bricks or a line of what looks like black felt. Any paving should be laid at least two courses of bricks below the damp course. If you don't do this, damp will rise up the walls and come into your house.

If you can't find the damp-proof course, you can leave a gap of about 20cm/8in out from the house and fill this with gravel; this allows water to drain, and prevents surplus water collecting next to the house walls. If you're in any doubt, consult the council or a qualified builder.

TOPOGRAPHY

Topography means the lie of the land, the localised geography of your particular area. Dramatic slopes and drastic changes in levels can be tricky, especially for the beginner. You might need to build terraces to accommodate a level seating area, and these might need retaining walls to hold back the weight of soil. These must be built properly, or they'll collapse – on to you and your guests, or your carefully planted garden! If you will be gardening on a dramatic slope I'd consult a professional before you start, unless, of course, you know exactly what you're doing.

The lie of the garden will also affect how rainwater drains away. If the ground slopes towards the house, the chance of flooding outside your back door is increased. Check your existing patio. Do large puddles form there? Does surface water drain from it towards the house? If so, your patio might need to be re-laid or replaced, with a different incline, so that surface water doesn't collect there or, more importantly, doesn't compromise the damp-proof course.

SOIL

Soils are made up of a mixture of sand, silt, clay and organic matter. The ratio of these elements varies, which is why some garden soils are naturally better for growing plants than others. Identifying your soil's texture and composition is useful, as these will affect how well it holds onto nutrients, how well it drains and how it behaves when you dig it. You don't need to major in soil science, or even carry out tests, but you do need to become familiar with the soil you've got.

Take a handful of moist soil from a couple of different places in the garden, and rub it between your fingers. If it feels gritty, doesn't stain the fingers, and doesn't easily form a ball... it's sandy soil. If it feels soapy, silky, 'squeaks' a bit, and dries into a fine dust... it's a soil with a high proportion of silt. A clay soil is easy to spot: sticky, smooth, shiny when you rub it between your thumb and forefinger, and easily forming a ball... very good for mud pies!

Ideally, what you want is an equal mixture of sand, silt and clay. This is the *pièce de résistance* of garden soils. Known as a loam, it combines the best attributes of each of the soil types, without too many of the nasty bits! But all soils can be improved – we'll look at how to do this later.

Right There is no better way to identify the type of soil you have than to handle it and assess its various characteristics.

SOIL TYPES

CLAY SOIL
Advantages
- Rich in plant food
- Holds water well, even in dry summers
- Loves organic matter

Disadvantages
- Wet and heavy in winter
- Bakes hard in summer
- Naturally cold, so takes time to warm up in spring
- Heavy and sticky, so hard to dig

SANDY SOIL
Advantages
- Easy to dig
- Warms up quickly in spring: good for early growth
- Loads of air: allows roots to grow strongly and deeply
- Drains well

Disadvantages
- Poor in nutrients: these 'leach', or wash out quickly
- Poor water retention: needs lots of organic matter added
- Can be very acidic: lime leaches out easily

THE ACID TEST

Getting a little technical here, but it's worth finding out the pH of your soil. This simply means how acid or alkaline it is. On a scale of 1 to 14, pH 1 is very acid, pH 14 very alkaline, with pH 7 being neutral. The ideal pH for most plants is 6.5, i.e. ever so slightly acid. To test your soil's pH you can buy a cheap little kit from any garden centre or DIY store. Follow the instructions on the back, and you'll soon know how acid or alkaline your soil is.

Most plants aren't that fussy about soil pH, but some, like rhododendrons, hate soils with a high pH (above 7): it contains too much lime. These acid lovers will sulk, even die, if you plant them in alkaline soil. Contrary to popular belief, you'll never be able to change the pH of your soil. So don't bother trying. If you want to grow acid lovers on an alkaline soil there's a simple solution. Grow them in pots filled with ericaceous (lime-free) compost!

EXISTING PLANTING

The hard landscaping makes up the bare skeleton of a design, but plants, especially the bigger ones, make up what I call the 'backbone' and give character, bulk and depth to your garden. If your space is bare you need to plant this layer first. If you've already got some mature plants, don't be too eager to remove them because replacements will take ages to reach maturity.

Keep choice evergreens especially, such as viburnum, the Mexican orange blossom (*Choisya ternata*), pittosporum, yew (*Taxus baccata*), or holly (*Ilex aquifolium*) for example. These are great for giving framework to any design.

VIEWS AND SURROUNDINGS
When doing your site survey, include the surroundings beyond your garden. Some features (like that gasometer) you'll want to screen. But there might be a church steeple or a city skyline that you could 'borrow' and incorporate into a design. It's a great way to have a magnificent focal point, unique to your garden.

Above left Make a cityscape view part of your garden by 'framing' it with plants.
Above If your soil is alkaline you can still grow acid-lovers such as camellias and rhododendrons. Simply pot them up in ericaceous compost and conceal the pot in your border.

Above A garden shed is almost indispensible for storing tools and materials such as plant pots and bags of compost.

the direction in which the pipes run. You'll then be able to avoid them or know where to take extra care when digging. Another obvious sign is subsidence or a different coloured strip of concrete in a driveway. Your local council should be able to help in these cases. They'll know the history of your property and have access to detailed maps and plans. You'll then easily be able to identify areas of your space where kid gloves are needed.

If the council can't help, and you're still worried, it's worth getting a small Cable Avoidance Tool (C.A.T.) from a local hire shop. It comes with instructions, but basically a C.A.T. is a hand-held sonar system: you walk over the soil with it and it tells you where any unmarked underground services are. Great fun! If you've got a balcony or roof terrace you can do the same, but using a cheap cable detector from any DIY store. Run it over the outside of your flat and mark where you find any cables. Alternatively find your sockets inside the house; cables to and from them usually run in straight horizontal or vertical lines, so outside you can trace on the wall where they're likely to be. Then at least you won't electrocute yourself when you're putting up a hanging basket!

WEIGHT PROBLEMS?

Weight is a factor to consider if you're gardening on a roof terrace or balcony. How much weight can your balcony actually take? It's pointless planting up loads of expensive containers, only to return home and find them sitting in the bathroom underneath where your roof terrace used to be! Usually the house survey or deeds will mention maximum weight, but if they don't, contact a surveyor or structural engineer who'll be able to advise you. It's also worth contacting the local planning department, especially if you're creating a new roof garden. You'll probably need planning permission – they're seen as an extra room.

GOING UNDERGROUND

Living in an urban environment invariably means that a multitude of cables and pipes are hiding underneath your garden, just waiting for you, the unsuspecting gardener, to pierce them with a fork or spade. Imagine hitting your cable-TV lead! What a nightmare: no TV for weeks, and it'll cost you a fortune. Fortunately most services are in protected cables and deep enough for you never to find them. But while the law states that contractors should lay cables at least 60cm/2ft deep, in my experience it's not always the case.

But don't worry. Finding underground services is easy, if you know where to look – here's where you get to play pretend-surveyor. The most obvious indicators are signs or inspection covers. Just lift up manholes and mark out on the ground

WATER SUPPLY

Think about installing an irrigation system. Every garden needs outside access to water, even if it's only an outdoor tap and a hosepipe – otherwise you'll end up having to fill and refill a watering can from inside the house, which can be a pain if you have lots of plants to soak. Fitting an outside tap won't take a good plumber longer than an hour, or you could do it yourself: just consult a DIY manual.

If a watering can sounds too time-consuming, there are numerous inexpensive systems at your local garden centre, from perforated seep hoses to micro sprinklers designed for lazy people like you and me. Some systems even have timers where you can programme your watering so that your plants get a soaking both morning and evening, while you're reading a book or supping a beer!

WINTER WONDERLAND

Don't ever garden just for the summer months. If you do, you'll be depressed for half the year, and you'll definitely miss out, especially as there are so many plants which look stunning in winter. Evergreens dominate the winter landscape. They give structure and cheer to the garden, and it's in this season that conifers really come into their own with their range of foliage colour from almost blue *Picea glauca* 'Caerulea' to deepest green. We begin to notice what we might have missed during all the fanfare of summer and autumn. The eye is hungry for shape and form because little is in flower, and on those grey winter days it seeks out the unusual. Complexity is summer's gift; the simplest shapes and muted colours belong to winter.

The winter garden is more subdued, apart from early bulbs in January and February, and yet it definitely has its own charm. This is the time to think about installing a garden sculpture which will act as a focal point. In summer a sculpture can be a surprise, half hidden by plants, but in winter a well-placed Japanese stone lantern, or an artful grouping of large, smooth pebbles, will have real interest and presence. Winter-interest plants should go near the house where you can see them from your windows. You might plant the climbing *Clematis cirrhosa* which has finely cut evergreen leaves and flowers in winter, or the winter jasmine (*Jasminum nudiflorum*) with its bright yellow starry flowers. Underplant these with bulbs such as snowdrops and crocus.

Some flowering shrubs will dominate the scene, like witch hazels (*Hamamelis*) with their curious spidery yellow or orange flowers that look like shredded ribbons and smell of marmalade. *Viburnum x bodnantense* 'Dawn' produces pinky-white clusters of fragrant flowers on bare wood. *Mahonia japonica* is an excellent evergreen backbone shrub in late winter. Its yellow flowers, shooting out from the foliage like open shuttlecocks, have a piercing scent of lily of the valley.

Pencil junipers (*Juniperus*) and clipped box (*Buxus*) look great in containers. Evergreen *Fatsia japonica* will survive happily if it's sheltered by a wall: ideal for an enclosed garden. Other plants of note for winter interest are *Skimmia laureola*, pyracanthas, *Rubus biflorus* (silver stems), the silk-tassel bush (*Garrya elliptica* – needs some protection but has gorgeous long catkins), *Choisya ternata* 'Sundance' for its sunny disposition, and wintersweet (*Chimonanthus praecox*) for its nodding, scented bellflowers. *Rosa rugosa* has giant hips which last the season. Bamboos still look smashing, although some lose their leaves in winter.

In autumn, remember to leave some seedheads for the winter garden: *Allium giganteum* with its large round heads, *Iris foetidissima* with its bright scarlet berries, *Achillea filipendulina* 'Gold Plate' with its flat yellow flowerheads, all retain winter interest, especially when dusted with frost, while *Bergenia* 'Ballawley' and *Euphorbia characias* add fine architectural detail.

Iris unguicularis will push up its scented blue-purple flowers when grown against a dry south-facing wall. It positively loves poor soil! *Malus hupehensis*, a crab apple, has red-tinged fruit which hang all winter. Bulbs such as winter aconites (*Eranthis*), snowdrops (*Galanthus*), crocus, *Iris reticulata* and early daffodils (*Narcissus*) can all be planted in great swathes under some of the duller backbone shrubs. The red stems of red-barked dogwood (*Cornus alba*) catch the low winter light, as does the bark of the cherry *Prunus serrula*, while *Prunus subhirtella* 'Autumnalis' actually flowers with delicate pinky-white blossom during mild winter spells – a real harbinger of spring. To get the best display of bright stems each year from *Cornus alba*, practise coppicing in the spring. This involves pruning back all stems right down to the ground, just when the first leaves start to appear; don't worry about such apparently drastic measures – people have been coppicing for centuries – and in this way you'll be promoting new growth while at the same time restricting the size of the shrub.

Pots of bulbs are a must; you can group these together where you'll be most likely to see them from a window. Most early flowerers don't kick in until mid-February, but if your garden is sheltered and the weather kind, many bulbs will put on an earlier display. In any case, the promise shown by bursting fresh green leaves and emerging leaves is exciting in itself.

Winter is also the time for whimsy and decoration. Make lanterns out of tin cans and string them up. Or use outdoor lights to run through a tree during dark December. Make a fire-pit or get the barbecue going. Light up your festivities by putting tiny candles in jars, setting them by a pathway. And lastly don't forget to hang bird-feeders out to bring in even more surprises!

1: *Hamamelis mollis* (Chinese witch hazel)
2: *Viburnum* x *bodnantense*
3: *Garrya elliptica* (silk-tassel bush)
4: *Bergenia* 'Ballawley' (elephant's ears)
5: *Rubus biflorus*
6: *Cornus alba* (red-barked dogwood)

GET TOOLED UP

Now's the time you might want to invest in some tools. Buy only what you actually need, not what you think you'll need in a few months. I have so many tools, I have no idea what half of them are for. But I guess they must have seemed like a good idea at the time!

The only essential tools you will need to start gardening with are a spade, a fork, a garden rake (or something that'll pull through the soil), a hand trowel and fork, a small pruning saw, a good quality pair of secateurs (ones you can sharpen easily) and, if you can accommodate it, a sturdy metal wheelbarrow. You might also want a pair of gardening gloves. If you find the need for other tools, then you can hire them. Many specialist shops will hire tools reasonably cheaply, and you don't have the worry of maintenance. Hiring is an ideal solution if you'll use a tool only rarely, or you've got no storage space.

If you are buying, spend a little more to get quality tools which should last you a lifetime. Make sure they're comfortable to use and easy to handle. For example, I often use a border spade (also known as a ladies' spade) because it's lighter, easier to handle, and I can do more work with it before getting knackered! I also like wooden handles: they have a nice feel, your hands don't stick to them if it's cold and if the handle breaks, it's easily replaced.

PUT IT DOWN ON PAPER

Questions ... questions ... I know. But they all need to be answered before you start implementing your ideas. That garden space must meet your functional needs as well as look great. There's little point in a visually spectacular garden if you can't actually use it properly. So get a list going. Circle those important requirements which you simply have to fit in. It'll help when you come to think about a design.

Once you've decided what you need, it's important to organise your thoughts so that you don't waste time, overlook important stuff or get in a flap. Grab a sketchpad and draw the location of the garden shed, the greenhouse (if you're lucky enough to have one, or the space for one), the compost bins and the washing line. Make sure that you site those items in constant use, like the rubbish bins, close to the door of your house or flat. You don't want to be wandering down the garden in the pouring rain to get rid of a stinking bag of fish bones! If you already have some idea where you want paths, a patio or some flower beds, mark them on too. You can always change the plan as your ideas take shape.

Above left The essential garden tool kit comprises just a few good quality tools which you will come to love. If storage space is limited, buy fold-up wheelbarrows.
Above Try out your layout ideas on the ground, using spray-on paint which is easily removed. Alternatively, you can trickle lines of sand. This will show whether you can fit in everything you want and whether the layout is working.

GET DOODLING!

If you're struggling to visualise quite where everything is going to go, loosen up and have some fun. Use your garden as a life-size doodle pad. Get hold of some spray-on paint or sand (something you can erase) and draw out on the ground where you want things to go. This will help you to visualise your ideas. If you aren't happy, rub out your markings and start again. Keep going until you're satisfied that everything works well together.

The orientation of your walls (which direction they face) is also important because it affects the range of plants you can grow against them. East-facing walls get a lot of sun in the morning but none in the late afternoon. West-facing fences and walls get the majority of their sun late afternoon and evening. The sides of directly north-facing walls and fences have perpetual shade, but those which face south usually get sun throughout the day – if they're not screened by a nasty office block! Grab a compass and take a couple of readings. It's that simple, and gets rid of any guesswork.

CITY LIGHTS, CITY SHADES

Every garden has a mixture of sunny and shady areas. It may broadly face north, for instance, but within that space the other compass points will also be there, and each area has its own particular character to consider when you come to plant.

Plants naturally seek out the light, just as we do, but in the city there are many obstructions to getting good light, whether it's neighbouring tall buildings or trees – or simply the fact that you live in a north-facing basement which is in shadow all the time.

Because we're a nation of sun-worshippers we think gardening should be an occupation enjoyed in the sun. And it's true that the brightest flowers do need the sun to look their best, just like we do! In practice we all devote more time and energy to sunny borders, while those in the shade tend to get neglected. True, plants which grow in shade aren't as spectacular as those sun-lovers, but they often have a subtle beauty. There are fine plants which love shade, need to grow there, and would die in the heat of a south-facing border. It's the contrasts which give the garden its vibrancy, and by devoting equal energy to all aspects, you'll have an outdoor room you can say is truly beautiful, right the way through! The secret is, as ever, matching the right plants to the right place.

IN PRAISE OF SHADE

We tend to see shade in the city as a problem; but only if we have too much of it. Actually, shade is vital. Think of a really hot day: after a while you find yourself looking for somewhere cooler to sit. That may be under the temporary shade of a parasol, or under a pergola covered by a climber. Sometimes we want to be right out of the sun, but at other times we simply like to have the force of its rays filtered by a floaty cotton awning overhead. It's certainly not difficult, if you have a south-facing garden, to put structures in place that will give you

Right It's still possible to grow a wide range of shade-loving plants under the natural shelter of trees.

shade when and where you want it. You might not have room for a trellised rose-walk, or an arbour covered with jasmine but in most gardens it's not too hard to find ways of modifying the sun's rays and creating shade.

For those of us who have nothing but shade, we have to find ways to make it dramatic and special. Shady gardens have something that sunny gardens simply don't – an atmosphere that can be quite other-worldly. Shady gardens can be full of mystery. Think of the mood of a grotto, with its ferns, mosses, water and silence: the intimacy of a cave. These places are often extremely relaxing. They may not have the loud Wow! factor of dramatic flower colour to shock you awake. Instead they rely on form, texture and a sense of intimacy. Shady places invite you to unwind in a different way. They are subtly seductive. My mother calls them places of the soul, whereas to her a sunny garden is a place of the senses.

SLIP-SLIDING AWAY

A word about hard landscaping in damp, shady conditions: don't use smooth paving materials. They quickly become mossy and slippery. Instead, go for textured bricks or slabs with some grip, or loose materials like gravel. Be aware that any sculptures, pots and stone or concrete walls will soon turn green with algae. This doesn't need scrubbing off; it's naturally caused by the wet and shade.

A thorough site evaluation will ultimately save you time and money

DEGREES OF SHADE

Dry shade might be your problem, caused by a large nearby tree whose roots suck up all the moisture from the soil. The wrong plants here will wither and die very quickly. In such a situation you won't be able to plant right up to the tree roots because it's too shady and too dry in summer. So forget it. The most you could grow would be ivy (*Hedera helix*) and dwarf periwinkles (*Vinca minor*). It is far better to live with what you've got, cherish the tree, and put a mulch of decorative bark underneath instead – and maybe fashion a circular bench round the trunk of the tree for lounging on.

Once trees are in full leaf they take centre stage, and nothing much else will happen until autumn when colchicums and cyclamens begin to flower underneath them. The male fern (*Dryopteris filix-mas*) will perk up then, too. Epimediums, with their heart-shaped leaves and tiny frothy flowers, will bronze attractively in autumn, and spread to give good ground cover. If you like galloping plants, try *Euphorbia robbiae*. And why not have scent with your shade – with Christmas box (*Sarcococca*) or *Skimmia laureola*?

If the shade in your garden is cast by a wall or fence, your plants are going to get more light and moisture throughout the year compared to those under a tree. Here you can have more flowering plants. *Anemone hupehensis* is a choice subject with its pure white or pink flowers on tall stems towering above elegant foliage. Although it's recommended as a plant for damp shade, it also grows superbly well in a dry south-facing border in my mum's garden. Some plants are very forgiving and will defy all the rules! Monkshood (*Aconitum*) is another choice, though poisonous, plant for damp shade with its spires of blue flowers, as are tree peonies (*Paeonia suffruticosa*), with bowl-like flowers in a range of colours.

ASPECT

In addition to the amount of shelter or the type of soil, each aspect – north, south, east, west – produces its own microclimate in your garden. That's why it's useful to go out with a compass and assess how your garden is orientated. On your rough plan, mark in the compass points.

NORTH-FACING

Let's say the back wall of your house faces directly north. This is probably where, if you have any soil at all, you'll have a sadly neglected border which slugs seem to love. You might think that nothing can be done to improve matters, but you would be wrong. First, be kind to your soil, adding lots of organic matter to give shade-loving plants a good start. Then do some research on exactly which plants will be happy there – and make a list of

those you intend to buy.

If you have a north-facing garden you'll be chasing the sun during the day, and may only come home to its western rays just before they disappear. And you may have a garden which is so enclosed with fencing and overgrown shrubs (not necessarily your own) that the sun barely filters in at all. This microclimate is one of perpetual shade. It's always cool in summer, and can get very cold in winter. Often the overhang of buildings or the roof eaves makes this even worse. If your garden faces north, but is fairly long, you'll get some sun at the bottom of it. If it's tiny, however, it may get little or no sun at all.

If you take this little microclimate out of the garden and transpose it into nature, the best approximation of these conditions would be a deep oak woodland, especially the dark, inner bits of the wood where you're scared to go! Or it might be at the bottom of the hill where the wood ends at a stream. You have two types of soil here: very dry under the trees, and wetter soil near the water – dry shade and wet shade.

Before the trees leaf up, a whole host of plants and bulbs flower and then die back, simply because there's more light during this time, and the plants are specialists at making full use of it! Bluebells (*Hyacinthoides non-scripta*) are a prime example, as are foxgloves (*Digitalis*) and the native mottled-leaved *Arum italicum*. These will do well in the garden, as will the white-flowered comfrey (*Symphytum grandiflorum*). Bulbs shine here, especially common snowdrops (*Galanthus nivalis*), dog's-tooth violets (*Erythronium dens-canis*), and very early daffodils (*Narcissus cyclamineus*). The purple-flowered self-heal (*Prunella grandiflora*) is one toughie that'll grow anywhere – I'll stake my reputation on it! You could also plant ferns, hostas, hardy cyclamen and even the morello cherry. For shrub cover try camellias, *Mahonia aquifolium*, cotoneasters and pyracanthas. If you want something to climb on a north-facing wall, try that old stalwart, the climbing hydrangea (*Hydrangea petiolaris*), or a honeysuckle (*Lonicera*).

Imagine a small, 5m/16ft square back yard in the city centre. It faces due north. Paint the walls white and position a huge mirror at one end to bring in extra light and make the place seem bigger. There is a ribbon of soil around the edges, so you grow most of the plants in large tubs and barrels. The garden does get a little sun, but barely enough. Plant an evergreen honeysuckle on the east wall with a huge *Fatsia japonica* at the base. Use variegated plants to bring brightness, like the silver-leaved *Euonymus* 'Silver Queen' and the gold-splashed *Elaeagnus pungens* 'Maculata'. Add a dwarf holly, as well as planting variegated ivy (*Hedera helix* 'Goldheart') everywhere. The planting will be mainly evergreen, giving year-round interest. *Viburnum davidii* with its electric blue berries and *Bergenia cordifolia* fill in the gaps, along with *Helleborus corsicus* and *H. orientalis*. We'll also manage to cram in a few herbaceous perennials such as *Viola cornuta*, the foam flower (*Tiarella cordifolia*), and bugle (*Ajuga reptans*). What I call the mouthful-plant – *Omphalodes cappadocica* – with its choice sprays of true blue flowers, fills the dampest spots. In summer we'll bring colour into the garden with hanging baskets full of busy lizzies (*Impatiens*) and fuchsias, their colours all the more vivid for not being bleached by the sun. Success is guaranteed if we work with what we've got.

HOSTAS

The entire hosta family has something to offer a shady garden. *Hosta sieboldiana* is the TV garden-designer's ally, with its spoon-shaped blue-green architectural leaves. *H. fortunei* 'Aurea' is almost lime green; *H. tardiana* 'Halcyon' is flushed with plum; *H.* 'Yellow Splash' does just what it says. Slugs love hostas, however, and can make a real mess of their neat leaves. If you grow them in containers you stand a better chance of escaping damage. I've heard that a strip of copper tape wrapped tightly around the pot will stop them climbing up: apparently the copper gives them an electric shock!

FERNS

For contrasts of texture and form in shady gardens, grow ferns. Versatile plants, many enjoy damp shady conditions, while some tolerate drier places. The downside is that they are quite expensive. Ferns suitable for drier conditions are the male fern (*Dryopteris filix-mas*) – sounds like the name of a dinosaur to me! – and the lady fern (*Athyrium filix-femina*). The hart's tongue fern (*Asplenium scolopendrium*) likes wet conditions, but you can also see it growing on west-country stone walls where it's very dry indeed! For wet spots plant the common polypody (*Polypodium vulgare*), or that beauty, the ostrich plume fern (*Matteuccia struthiopteris*), which throws up perfect shuttlecocks of pale green.

Above left The ostrich plume fern (*Matteuccia struthiopteris*) survives even a boggy spot, and the feathery fronds are highly attractive.
Left *Hosta sieboldiana* has fantastic blue-green architectural leaves and lilac flower spikes.

EAST-FACING

Walls facing east might have to cope with bitter winds and extremes of temperature. The earth here is generally cool, liable to get dry in summer and freeze in winter. Evergreens planted in this area can get badly frost-damaged. This is rather a bleak aspect, and even in the urban environment can be wind-swept and unforgiving. The equivalent in nature would be an exposed area such as you might find when you come out of the eastern side of a wood, and encounter the type of land called, rather unattractively, scrub.

Plants which will withstand these conditions include many in the north-facing group. You'd be surprised, but some roses do rather well too. That's because they are tough old stems in winter, and by the time they leaf up and flower the weather is hopefully kinder. If you want to grow camellias, this is another aspect which suits them, but naggingly you have to shade the flowers from early morning sun if it's frosty, otherwise they blacken. Carefully sited, the camellia is a superb half-barrel subject (it likes acid soil), and its scentless brilliantly coloured flowers seem so at odds with the weather that they could be exotics imported from hotter climates! Cheering hellebores are tough old things,

too, and architectural with it. Forget the Christmas rose (*Helleborus niger*), so beloved of slugs and slow to get going, and go for *Helleborus orientalis* instead, with flowers of purple, plum and soft reds.

WEST-FACING

West-facing walls, or their equivalent, have a kind temperament with lots of afternoon sun. They give plants fairly warm conditions in which to grow, with none of the extremes of north- or south-facing walls. These conditions are similar to those on the edge of woodland, colonised by plants that don't like blistering sun all day.

Many plants grow well on a western aspect, especially the more tender ones which need cosseting. The list is numerous and includes most of the herbaceous perennials. Lilies do well, as do most jasmines, Californian lilac (*Ceanothus*), *Clematis armandii*, daphnes and viburnums – all choice plants. Annuals seem to thrive in this aspect, and aren't over as quickly as when they are grown in a south-facing border. The west-facing aspect is the gardener's friend, a good place to have a seating area tucked away among scented plants. It's the place to chill and watch your plants as the sun slowly sinks.

Below Tailor your planting according to which part of the garden gets the most sun and where the shadiest spots are – a sun-loving plant won't thank you if it only sees the sun for ten minutes each day!

SOUTH-FACING

This aspect means an extreme microclimate. This is the favoured site for planting specimens which need a kinder winter, like the classy wintersweet (*Chimonanthus praecox*). Many plants will survive planted against south-facing walls that would die in the open garden. Plants exposed to the southern sun can get very hot in summer, causing scorch on leaves and drought at the roots. But with retentive soil you can grow many more than just those which thrive in Mediterranean countries. Lavender, rosemary and all the silver- and grey-leaved shrubs love the heat. Think of a Grecian hillside. Rock plants and those with fleshy leaves like the houseleeks (*Sempervivum*) will also do well. The nice thing about sun-lovers are the flowers, which can be as exotic as red and yellow cannas or as brilliant as a scarlet geranium. Crinums, *Amaryllis belladonna*, african lilies (*Agapanthus*) and nerines will love the sun and shelter!

KICKING UP A FUSS

You can usually get away with planting something in a southerly aspect that's recommended for a west-facing one. You can also plant a shrub on an east-facing wall that'll do nicely on a north-facing one. What you can't do is take a fussy plant which likes only full sun and then plant it in full shade, or vice versa, because you'd force the plant to cope with an extreme it can't tolerate. A fern that specifically needs a bog garden will shrivel and die on a south-facing wall. But I have seen pots of scarlet geraniums in sunless basements – it depends on how fussy the plants are. You have to experiment. Some people who have basement gardens actually put their geraniums on a sunny kitchen windowsill for a day or so each week to stock up on sun. Better to grow busy lizzies (*Impatiens*) here, though. These must be the most vivid floriferous plant out, yet they don't mind a sunless aspect. That's gardening!

KNOWING YOUR PLANTS

WHAT MAKES THEM TICK?

In order for plants to grow they need the right environment. This includes a good water supply, unpolluted air, light, nutrients, a suitable temperature and good soil. You've probably grown

many plants with the minimum of care and attention – a bit of fertiliser here, a splash of water there – but if you take time to find out their individual requirements, what you'll grow will be worthy of applause.

The plant world is full of incredible diversity and even within the same genus (family) you're likely to find varieties with totally different soil and site preferences and growing requirements. Take clematis, for example. Early-flowering species such as *Clematis montana* 'Elizabeth' prefer north- or east-facing walls – those shaded for a large proportion of the day – whereas some of its large, late-flowering counterparts, such as *Clematis* 'Ernest Markham', love sites in full sun. Yet, as with all clematis, both varieties need to have their roots in the shade and their heads in the sun.

Part of a gardener's job to is appreciate that while plants may have similar general requirements they also have specific ones as well. Take my lilies as an example. My balcony gets full sun – and I mean full sun. Sometimes it's so hot I can't stand on it barefoot, but I could fry an egg on it! My balcony is no place for a faint-hearted plant. But because I've evaluated the site, recognising both the good and bad things, I have an intuitive feeling about when my lilies are happy and when they need some additional shade, a drink of water or a dose of tomato fertilizer (one of the best foods for flowering plants, by the way). You'll get the same feeling, I guarantee! Just give your plants daily

Above African lilies, with their rounded flowerheads held on elegantly tall stems, enjoy a sunny, south-facing aspect – and the dead flowers will provide interest in winter.

Full sun/sun-loving	Plants that prefer a really sunny position, ideally in a south- or west-facing aspect. Avoid locations that are consistently shaded by trees and buildings.
Prefers partial shade or half-shade	Plants that prefer partial shade typically come from the edge of woodlands, where they get filtered sunshine. Avoid sunny, hot sites – the plants will cook. Perfect in west-facing locations or sites shaded by buildings or trees for part of the day.
Shade-loving/shade-tolerant	Shade-loving plants will usually cope with the deepest of shade – underneath trees, next to walls, underneath man-made structures or in north-facing locations. Most shade-tolerant plants will benefit from a little sunshine, but it's not essential.
Suitable for dry shade	Plants suited to areas shielded from the rain – underneath trees or next to boundaries and house walls. If it says dry shade on the label the plant will probably grow anywhere!
Ideal for wet shade	Plants for wet sites – next to water, in a bog garden or at the bottom of sloping gardens, shielded by trees, man-made structures or buildings.
Suitable for exposed sites	Plants for areas exposed to the elements, where excessive wind may be a problem. Ideal for balconies and roof terraces.
Suitable for coastal sites	Plants suitable for windswept coastal locations where salt air may damage more tender plants.
Suitable for polluted sites	Perfect plants for the true urban gardener. Ideal for heavily polluted gardens, roof terraces or balconies, next to busy roads or in the centre of cities.

attention. It doesn't take long. You'll soon be able to recognise when they're unhappy. That's the reason I don't have a self-watering system, but prefer to water by hand. It gives me the chance to get up close and personal.

COMMON CARE TERMS

Most gardening retail outlets identify the plants they sell with labels naming the particular variety, and also often describing where it's suitable to grow them and whether they have any specific requirements. If the seller doesn't provide any of the above, I'd head for the exit – if they can't be bothered to provide such basic information it's doubtful whether they've shown a lot of care growing the plant. However, if you do find yourself with a plant that you've no idea how to care for, all is not lost – just do a bit of research and look it up in a plant directory (the one in the final chapter of this book makes a good starting point!). The table above will help you to understand the care terms that most commonly crop up on plant labels, seed packets and gardening books.

LIFE-CYCLES

What makes a plant tick – its preferred growing conditions – is just one way of thinking about plant types. Another is to consider the way in which plants grow: the different life-cycles they have and the type of growth they make. Some plants will grow from seed, put on foliage and stems, produce flowers, then seeds again, before wilting and dying – all within a year. For others the life-cycle takes two years, or it's only the top growth that dies and the plant will sprout again in the spring, while others stay permanently green. If you know that a plant is only supposed to live for a year, or that it dies down only to grow back in the spring, then you won't get upset wondering what you did wrong – and, more importantly, you won't dig up a plant that is just pretending to be dead!

ANNUALS

Annuals only live for a year. The seed germinates, flowers, sets more seed, and dies, all within 12 months. The flowers planted in pots and hanging baskets, or in traditional 'summer bedding'

arrangements, tend to be annuals or exotic tender perennials grown as annuals. Many garden weeds, such as meadow grass and willow herb, are annuals, which means they can be put on the compost heap but only before they have set seed.

Half-hardy annuals won't tolerate hard frosts. They must be grown under cover and planted out after the danger of frost has gone (typically late May). Most summer bedding plants such as lobelia, bedding geraniums (*Pelargonium*), snapdragons (*Antirrhinum*) and French marigolds (*Tagetes*) are half-hardy annuals, as are some vegetables such as runner beans and courgettes. Half-hardy annuals are typically used to give a splash of colour in flower beds or hanging baskets. However, they must be replaced each spring and this can be expensive.

Hardy annuals tolerate frost, and their seeds can be planted in the winter. Among the most popular hardy annuals are: pot marigolds (*Calendula officinalis*), cornflower (*Centaurea cyanus*), California poppy (*Eschscholzia californica*), clarkia and mallow (*Lavatera trimestris*).

BIENNIALS

Plants such as foxgloves (*Digitalis*), Canterbury bells (*Campanula medium*), and sweet William (*Dianthus barbatus)* have a two-year life-cycle and are known as biennials. These are generally sown in late summer. In the first year the plant puts on leaves and stems, and in the second it flowers, sets seed and dies. In warmer locations some biennials don't

actually die after two years, but will continue to flower year after year, if a little less well.

PERENNIALS

Perennials are plants that live longer than two years and normally flower annually. Garden weeds like brambles, couch grass, horsetail, ground elder and bindweed are perennials – and don't we know it!

Half-hardy perennials will survive average winter conditions, but only in sheltered positions. However,

Far left The banana plant (*Musa basjoo*) is a good example of a tender perennial that can survive the winter if given protection. It brings an exotic touch to a city garden.
Left Cornflowers (*Centaurea cyanus*) are beautiful annuals and make a great addition to any planting scheme, or can be planted in blue drifts on their own.
Below The biennial sweet William (*Dianthus barbatus*) has a two-year life-cycle. Plant them in late summer and you should see some growth in year one, followed by strong colour in year two.

Annual	Plants with a life-cycle of one year. Annuals are either hardy or half-hardy
Half-hardy annual	Annual plants which cannot tolerate very low temperatures. Plant out after the last frosts have passed.
Hardy annual	Annual plants tolerant of frosts. Can be sown or planted out during winter and early spring.
Biennial	Plants with a two-year life-cycle. Leaves and stems grow in the first year, flowers and seeds in the second. Generally sown in late summer.
Perennial	Plants living for more than two years, usually flowering each year. Half-hardy perennials may not survive the winter in colder parts of the country.
Herbaceous perennial	Perennial plants whose top growth dies back in the winter but grows again in spring. Generally, remove dead foliage to encourage new growth.
Tender exotic	Perennial plants originating from warmer climates which need protection from low temperatures.
Broad-leaved tree	Woody perennial plants, generally single-stemmed, which drop their leaves in winter.
Conifer	Shrubs or trees which are usually cone-bearing and evergreen.
Shrub	Evergreen or deciduous woody plants, smaller than trees and often with many stems originating from the base.
Houseplant	Perennials from exotic climates, traditionally grown indoors as they are unlikely to withstand low temperatures.

it's worth remembering that geographical location – the climate where you live – can also play its part. Half-hardy perennials will survive winters in areas that never have long periods of frost, but not in places that have below average temperatures most of the time.

Herbaceous perennials live for longer than two years, but the top growth dies back in winter to re-emerge in spring. Growth is typically soft but some may turn slightly woody towards the end of the season. Lady's mantle (*Alchemilla mollis*), Christmas rose (*Helleborus niger*), delphinium, hardy geranium, *Phlox maculata*, *P. paniculata* and *Rudbeckia* 'Herbstsonne' are all herbaceous perennials. Usually you remove dead foliage and stems in early spring to encourage new shoots.

Tender perennials tend to be classed as exotic, such as Indian shot (*Canna*) and banana (*Musa*). They can actually be considered as half-hardy

perennials, as they are capable of living through the winter if they're given protection. 'Exotic' is another term for describing half-hardy perennials that are a bit on the fancy side!

TREES AND SHRUBS

All trees are woody perennials, having a permanent branch structure and usually a single stem. Deciduous trees lose their leaves in winter. Broadleaved examples include the horse chestnut (*Aesculus hippocastanum*), Japanese maples (*Acer palmatum* and *japonicum*) apples (*Malus*), birches (*Betula*) and hawthorn (*Crataegus*).

Conifers are usually cone-bearing trees or shrubs, such as Scots pine (*Pinus sylvestris*) and Norway spruce (*Picea abies*). The Leyland cypress (x *Cupressocyparis leylandii*) is also classed as a conifer even though it has no cones and therefore no seeds. Most conifers are evergreen and are usually typified by their needle-like leaves.

Shrub is a generic term loosely used to describe relatively small to medium-sized woody plants that can be either evergreen or deciduous. Unlike trees, which usually have a single stem originating from the base, shrubs typically have many stems. Common shrubs include the butterfly bush (*Buddleja*), Californian lilac (*Ceanothus*), rosemary (*Rosmarinus*), and French lavender (*Lavandula stoechas*).

HOUSEPLANTS

This is a loose term for those plants which aren't hardy in our climate. In fact, many are actually half-hardy or will grow outside quite happily during the summer months but must be brought inside before the first frosts. In the tropics, where there are no extremes of cold, houseplants such as the rubber plant (*Ficus elastica*) and the spider plant (*Chlorophytum*) thrive outdoors.

GETTING STUCK IN

Once you've gone through the laborious but essential process of evaluation, it's time to take action. If you've found any underground services make sure they're clearly marked, then set about clearing all the rubbish. It might be worth hiring a skip, or you could bag up any debris, put it in the car and drive it to the local municipal recycling centre. Don't bother to hire a van, however, as many refuse stations will charge you trade rates. If you're going to transport rubbish through the house, lay down heavy dustsheets so that you don't damage any flooring or carpets. If you have a large quantity of woody materials you could burn it, following all safety procedures for bonfires.

CREATING A BLANK CANVAS

First get rid of anything you don't like, including weeds, glass, rubbish and the all-too-common builder's rubble. But before you throw out bricks, timber, chimney pots, metalwork, paving slabs etc, think carefully. You might be able to recycle them in your new design. Many existing features in urban gardens have loads of character and make a garden look older and more authentic. If you decide you don't want to keep them, however, take a sample to a local reclamation yard – they might offer to buy your cast-offs from you and come and collect them!

Now's the time to replace bad fencing. Remember always to work from the outside of your plot towards the middle, otherwise you will only be trampling over your newly planted garden. If the lawn is in fairly good shape, keep it. Decking or

Above left French lavender (*Lavandula stoechas*) is a popular sun-loving shrub that is more commonly thought of as a flower. It's great for adding colour and scent, and is popular with bees too.
Above *Ceanothus arboreus* 'Trewithen Blue' is a brilliant shrub for adding colour and attracting birds and insects.

Above, left to right Getting stuck into a garden that's been allowed to go wild can be a daunting task. Be prepared for some physical exertion, but keep thinking about the final rewards – and the beer you can rightly allow yourself!

hard surfaces may appeal, but lawns can be cut into sculptural shapes, too.

Take a good look at the trees. Are they just in need of some TLC, or do some need felling? Before you get out the chain saw, ask yourself whether the trees contribute to the 'architecture' of the garden? Will the pruning or felling of a healthy conifer suddenly reveal the electricity sub-station next door? And before you attack any tree, saw in hand, ask yourself if you're qualified to do the job. If you have a big tree you must check with the council to see whether it has a Tree Preservation Order on it. Any tree work ideally needs the services of a professional tree surgeon: ask your council for a recommendation. Avoid cowboy firms working from the side of the road, with ladders strapped to the sides of enormous trees, the vans covered with lurid luminous script! Go to the professionals and ask for a visit and a quote. Cowboys simply don't know what they're doing!

THE CHEMICAL QUESTION

If your garden's overflowing with weeds, you need to clear them. Do you do this by hand or do you resort to chemicals? Hand weeding is laborious, while chemicals are quicker. But are they safe? And are they ethical?

Currently, there is nothing more likely to cause vehement debate within the horticultural world than the chemical question. Many people (especially my mum!) have had enough of chemicals, though they're routinely applied to commercial crops and livestock. Who knows the cumulative effects of this chemical cocktail? One thing's for sure. If they kill bugs and weeds on contact, they're not going to be totally harmless to us! And if you read the back of any chemical bottle it'll say things like, 'harmful to bees' or 'harmful to aquatic life' – that's not very cool sprayed all over your garden.

If you're a beginner, or concerned about the environment, play safe. Go organic and only use chemicals where absolutely necessary. If you've got children or pets, don't use chemicals. Simple. Instead, hire a flame gun from your hire shop and go over the whole garden. This will kill a lot of weeds on contact. Those which survive you can either dig up, or (especially in the case of perennial weeds like bindweed, couch and elder) apply a spot weed killer directly to the leaves. This isn't a spray, but a contact weed killer.

An even better, and thoroughly sociable, way of getting rid of weeds without chemicals or flame-throwers is to invite some friends round. Have a barbecue, crack open a couple of beers and goad them into helping you weed your space by hand. It's so much safer, and you'll sleep better knowing that you haven't contaminated your garden before you've even started!

Be prepared to get down and dirty!

Above There is no better soil improver than a barrow-load of well-rotted horse manure – or home-made garden compost – spread over the soil and dug or forked into the top layer.

DEALING WITH THE SOIL

If your house is new, or you've neglected the garden, the chances are that your soil won't be in pristine condition. Unfortunately, many of the soils we're likely to have will either be too free-draining, easily waterlogged, or bake themselves hard in summer. Despite this, most soils will still support growing plants, but it's equally true to say that most soils could allow the plants to grow better. With a little work, your soil could be so good it'll be almost edible! I'm generally a lazy gardener, but I still spend a lot of time tending my soil because I know it's important and good for the long term.

WHAT TO DIG OUT

Once your soil is free of weeds, dig it over. If you come across a lot of yellow builder's sand, dig it

out and get rid of it. This kind of sand is full of lime, which will radically alter the pH of your soil (unlike horticultural sand). You might also find sand like this under an old patio or path.

If you find any oil spilt on the earth, again dig it out. It's like sulphuric acid to plants, and will kill them. Also check that your soil hasn't been turned over. No, I don't mean robbed! But if your house was recently built, it may have had strangely coloured subsoil dumped on top of your lovely topsoil. Plants don't like to grow in old subsoil! Dig down carefully and see if there's decent topsoil (which will be a darker colour) buried underneath it. If you find some you'll have to shovel away the stuff on the top – poor you!

DIG OVER AND DIG IN

Once you've cleared the soil and have got some adequate topsoil, before planting anything you first need to dig it over to a spade's depth. Take it slowly, and it won't seem such a chore. This initial digging breaks up the soil, aerates it, and throws up pests to the surface to be eaten by birds. It's at this stage that you should also dig in some soil improvers to increase fertility and improve the structure – unless you reckon your soil doesn't need it. But in my experience there's always room for improvement!

The best route to take when it comes to improving your soil involves my favourite stuff: fresh organic compost. I can't over-emphasise how good organic matter is for soil and plants. It improves and maintains good soil structure, aids drainage on clay and silty soils, and improves the water-holding capacity of sandy soils. Organic matter basically feeds the soil and provides everything that both plants and beneficial soil organisms need.

Get hold of whatever you can locally: chicken manure, horse manure, spent hops, spent mushroom compost – you could even ask your greengrocer to save his throw-away veggies in a sack or two for you to collect. This will make fantastic garden compost mixed in with your own kitchen waste and the odd shredded newspaper. When it's matured into a crumbly texture ('friable' is the gardening term) and no longer smells, which takes from three to six months, it's ready for the garden. The best way to use this precious resource is to spread it over the soil and gently fork it into the top 5cm/2in. The worms will do the rest of the digging for you, pulling the compost down to deeper levels where the nutrients become available to plant roots. You can dig it in deeper but, if you're pressed for time or have a bad back, don't worry. Nature is on your side. Adding a load of lovely compost improves the structure of the soil, making it more friable so that it will crumble satisfyingly.

CREATING THE RIGHT SPACE FOR YOU

Having surveyed and cleared your site, it's time to get down to design: the fun part. Your head will be full of ideas, and most of them will be too ambitious – we're all the same! Try to think simple; don't plump for something really adventurous or difficult that will require professional help, unless you really don't want to get your hands dirty and plan on employing a garden designer anyway.

One of the hardest things to persuade any beginner gardener to do is be patient. I'm still trying to preach patience to myself. Gardens are continually evolving and they never actually reach a state where you can say, 'There, finished!' So don't rush out with the intention of completing a grandiose project in a weekend. Take as much time as you can – and enjoy the experience.

Below There's renewed interest in naturalistic, relaxed planting designs inspired by the traditional cottage garden.

CHOOSING THE RIGHT DESIGN

Garden design is a modern concept which goes with today's lifestyle. There are many books and schools of opinion on 'the right design'. It seems that everybody has something to say on the subject, which makes it confusing for the first-time gardener. And what one expert loves, another gently ridicules. So garden design is a fickle business, always seeking out new trends. In reality, there are very few completely new concepts out there. Many designs are recycled or re-interpreted ideas which gardeners have been using for ages. As in the fashion industry, these pop up every few years as the next big thing!

Not so long ago, there was a fashion for modernist or minimalist gardens with lots of hard landscaping and concrete and hardly a plant in sight. Some of these pushed to the limits our concept of what a garden should be. New materials surfaced, like coloured glass and shiny metals, and any plants were almost secondary considerations, useful for softening the starkness of these designs. If you go to any of the major flower shows and look at the small garden exhibits, you'll see many such gardens and some of them I'll admit are visually stunning 'set pieces' – but is that really what gardening is all about? Perhaps if you are an avant-garde stage set designer!

Left You'd have thought glass blocks would be out of place in a garden, yet strangely there's a natural affinity between the glass and the lawn – as if the glass is mimicking pools of water.

But recently there has been a move back to more naturalistic gardens with a cottagey feel where the planting is softer, more relaxed. People now want a little piece of the country in their back yards: a reminder of an old-fashioned and more comforting time, perhaps.

I think there's a place for both 'modern' and 'traditional' gardens – even a successful marriage between the two. To a certain extent this has already happened, with the advent of decking and cobalt blue paintwork! In the 1970s, when just about everyone wanted a patio, they appeared in suburban gardens almost overnight, complete with crazy paving. We still have patios, but have now also introduced many different types of materials, allowing us to mix and match and experiment with texture. Bricks, cobbles, gravel and stone may be used in close proximity, visually complementing each other, perhaps with spaces left for plants where the different materials meet.

BASIC DESIGN PRINCIPLES

When it comes down to it, design is all about personal taste. But there are a few basic principles to bear in mind, the most important of which is: aim for simplicity! Try not to use too many different features and materials, as they tend to make a small space look fussy. A path which employs more than three different materials looks odd next to an intricate planting scheme; two overly 'busy'

areas will fight each other for attention. I appreciate that simplicity is difficult to achieve, especially if you've a garden the size of a postage stamp and still want to have a pond, a patio, a barbecue and a shed. You might have to choose to do without something – the jacuzzi, for example! The result will be a less congested, more relaxing space that's easier on the eye.

You'll want to create a sense of harmony both within the garden and between the garden and the house. Try to view your garden as a whole, otherwise it'll look chaotic and disorganized. This doesn't mean you can't divide it into 'rooms', but that you should endeavour to link all the areas together smoothly. Unity could be achieved by using the same hedging throughout, by repeating certain plants in each area or by using a paving material that matches the house. Repeating shapes or plants – whether it's foliage, flowers or colour – will help everything to harmonise. But there's absolutely nothing wrong with an eclectic mix of styles or materials. Stepping from a timber deck to granite setts and gravel provides a great contrast in texture – just make sure that the transition from one to the other is smooth, feels natural and isn't jarring.

It's also important to achieve a harmony of size and shape. I'm sure everybody has seen an enormous lawn with a tiny island bed in the middle of it, or window boxes overflowing with enormous shrubs. They're out of proportion and just don't look right. Similarly, large paving slabs might dwarf a small garden, whereas small clay pavers are more in scale. Check the proportions of your features against each other and within the garden as a whole once you've marked them out – it'll be obvious when it looks right. Avoid collecting features on only one side of the garden or your space will lack balance and look lopsided.

As well as the hard landscaping, the shape of flower beds and paths needs to feel right. Free-form shapes and sweeping curves create a dynamic sense of movement, more appropriate to a large space, perhaps. Regular geometric shapes – circles, squares and rectangles – are suited to small gardens with strong, straight boundaries.

Below Unity is achieved in this garden by using bricks as edging for both the gravel path and the paving stones in the foreground – it ties the whole design together.

ESTABLISHING A BUDGET

If you haven't already done so, you'll need to work out a budget for your new garden. As well as the plants and hard-landscaping materials, you'll need to include hidden costs such as skip hire, tool hire and tree surgeons, as appropriate. It's a good idea to first cost the things you need, like a shed or a seating area, and then factor in other desirable features such as arches, arbours and focal points – features you could do without if the budget starts to rocket. Add in some contingency cash as well, then if you hit a problem you'll have spare money set aside to deal with it.

At this point you may consider employing a professional garden designer to help with the planning. But for most people this is an unnecessary additional cost. It's true they may be able to save you time and hassle, but it shouldn't be necessary if you're approaching your project carefully. And surely you want the kudos of planning the garden yourself! However, if you still think you need the help of a professional, make sure you get several quotes first.

For costing hard-landscaping materials, check out DIY stores as well as builder's merchants. DIY outlets may have a limited selection but they are generally cheaper. If you want something a little more specialised, visit a stone mason or a timber merchant; you'll find an enormous range of materials, which will be excellent value because these merchants purchase in bulk and can pass on the savings to the customer. Such specialist outlets will also be able to help with the construction techniques involved in laying a patio, for example, to augment the information you will find in basic 'How to' books at the library.

For certain designs, materials that look slightly weathered and worn-in are preferable. New paving slabs often look too suited, booted and clean-shaven for a period or cottage-style garden. For second-hand materials reclamation yards are a goldmine, stocking everything from wrought iron to railway sleepers, from chimney pots to glassware. A good search might reveal a gem of an unusual statue or planter. In the past few years, however, reclamation yards have received a lot of media coverage and have put up their prices as a result, so be prepared to fight for a good deal.

Bear in mind as you're clearing the site of the existing garden area, that you might find older materials lying about which could be incorporated into the design. Often you'll unearth dozens of old bricks, the remnants of a wall or out-house which has since disappeared. Whatever you do, don't chuck them in a skip! Dust them down and they'll look fantastic as edging or a bit of hard surfacing to place pots on. You're also incorporating a part of the old garden into your new design.

By now you've probably realised that plants are my thing. But don't let my enthusiasm fool you. Hard landscaping (the 'skeleton') also has a vital practical and aesthetic role in any design. What is 'hard landscaping'? The term is used to encompass any non-living feature in the garden, including patios, steps, paths, walls, fences or pergolas. The hard landscaping holds a design together, and the type of materials and features you select will dramatically alter the appearance and character of the garden.

When you're thinking about the hard stuff, try and keep in mind the garden's living framework – the position of trees, shrubs and hedges. Plants will dramatically affect the style of your garden – whether it be formal, with the use of clipped hedges, or informal, with curved beds overflowing with herbaceous perennials. My real quarrel with hard landscaping is that it's so often over-elaborate, costing a fortune, or else it's impractical and means the garden can't be used properly. Arriving at the right design is all about finding a happy medium between the hard stuff and the soft (the plants). However, if I had a choice between building a screening wall (all that preparation, cost and hard work), or planting a stunning golden-coloured honey locust tree (*Gleditsia triacanthos* 'Sunburst'), to do the same job – no contest!

CHOOSING SURFACE MATERIALS

Spend as much money as you are able to on paved areas and paths. They might initially be expensive, but they make up the core of a design, so their appearance will affect everything around them. There are many surfacing materials to choose from: natural stone, pre-cast concrete slabs, bricks, ceramic tiles, granite and sandstone setts, metal, timber, glass, plastic, gravel, grass and bark. Whatever surface you decide upon, it must be functional and durable. And when you select a material, try to make sure it's in keeping with the style of your garden: concrete and metal might easily look out of place in a natural style garden, whereas granite setts and weathered bricks would suit it perfectly.

Paving materials can be expensive and what you can't see must also considered: the hardcore base, the foundations, the hidden drainage and perhaps the cost of specialist advice. However, a little innovation in combining materials can ease the financial burden without spoiling the overall effect – expensive granite may be interspaced with cheaper railway sleepers, for example. Similarly, if you're using concrete, which is relatively cheap, incorporate swirling lines of cobbles to add interest and class to an otherwise monotonous material.

SEATING AREAS

Materials used to floor a seating area generally need to be solid, not loose and flexible like pebbles and large-grade gravel. Natural stone, timber and pre-cast concrete slabs are ideal, but for heavy use the latter need an extra firm base and careful

Above left Bricks laid in a traditional herringbone pattern.
Above right Slate is one of the few surface materials that looks even better in the rain.
Left Hard landscaping is probably the trickiest and most labour-intensive aspect of gardening, but you only need to do it once (or once in a while) and then you can devote all your time to plants!

Above left Solid, dependable stone slabs for that classic, already-weathered look.

Above centre Pebbles make a satisfyingly crunchy texture under foot.

Above right Metal steps have an industrial feel to them, but they could look fantastic in an ultra-modern, minimalist garden.

Right Laying small-grade gravel over an existing solid surface is one way to spruce up a seating area, without spending lots of money.

Right below Turf is ideal for visual effect or as a child-friendly surface, but it won't easily accommodate a table and chairs.

laying if they aren't to crack or shift. The surface needs to be flat and reasonably level, but with a gentle slope falling away from the house so that surface water doesn't gather in a puddle or compromise the damp-proof course. If your seating area is not adjacent to the house, you might need a hard path leading to it. Using the same materials helps to create a sense of continuity throughout.

When choosing materials for paths, steps and seating areas, take into account the direction your garden faces. Natural stone and timber are perfect materials for full sun, but they can easily become slippery in winter or in the shade of buildings and trees, making them treacherous underfoot. Bricks, granite setts and textured concrete slabs all give better grip in such conditions.

LAWNS

Grass doesn't make the best seating area. Lawns are fine for lying around in deck chairs or sun-loungers, but they don't easily accommodate a table and chairs, except in really dry weather. For visual effect, however, or if you've got kids and need a safe, low-cost material for them to play on, a lawn is ideal. While hard materials are more functional, lawns are far cheaper, regardless of whether you establish them by laying turf or sowing seed. As for maintenance, just mow it once a week in summer: this will help keep the weeds out and make a lovely thick green carpet – what could be simpler? If you are likely to use the garden predominantly in summer, then grass will give a soft surface to sunbathe on and will still provide a visually attractive surface in winter.

PATHS

Almost any material can be used for a path, but gravel is one of my favourites. Among the cheapest of all hard-surfacing materials, it's also one of the easiest to lay and ideal for covering a large area. There are many decorative gravels available in all sizes and colours, with wonderful names such as Gaelic marble, Cotswold stone, Welsh slate, weathered flint, Trent pink and Nordic spar, all of which will provide a foil for some well thought-out planting. Gravel is cool because it has such a lovely crunchy sound, which makes it perfect for the security conscious. I really love the fact that you can grow plants through it, making it an ideal material for informal designs as the path becomes part of the flower beds.

Paths made of loose aggregate may need an edge to stop the gravel spreading over the garden. They'll also need the occasional top up, but at least they won't need sweeping regularly. Weed growth shouldn't be a problem as long as you first lay a semi-permeable membrane (available at garden centres and DIY stores) and then put a 2.5cm/1in deep layer of gravel on top. Timber railway sleepers laid across a gravel path can add a contrasting texture and help to hold the loose aggregate in place, but also demand that you stop and look at the planting on either side. If you lay sleepers along the direction of the path, they hint at a focal point ahead, encouraging you to move along the path more quickly.

If you're going for a contemporary look, steel or aluminium grids are good materials, especially for steps. Unfortunately they often have to be specially made to fit the space, so can be expensive. Used sparingly throughout a garden, they'll help reflect light as well as giving a very cool, modern ambience to the garden. However, in full sun you might find that glare is a problem.

Glass gravel is worth considering to brighten up a shady space, perhaps used as infill between timber log slices. In a sunny garden it'll set off dazzling flares and, used under water, will sparkle like precious stones.

Mosaic paths are a satisfying surface which you can construct yourself. The pattern you choose is limited only by your imagination. On a large scale, laying mosaics is very time consuming, but a little detail running through a brick path, or emphasising the base of a statue, is far less work and can look absolutely stunning. Mosaics are easy to create – just set pieces of different coloured slate, pebbles, marbles, beads, cobbles, up-turned wine bottle ends or shells into wet concrete. Mosaic-making is a great way to get the whole family involved in a garden project.

A well thought-out path can also help to alter perspective. Long, straight paths accentuate a narrow garden, whereas a twisting path running from side to side across a garden creates an illusion of width. If your garden is wide, taper your path the further it recedes down the garden; narrowing it in this way will give the illusion of length, as though the path was disappearing into the distance. Have a practice in the garden with some sand or spray-on line, and you'll be amazed how the simplest change in path direction will affect the feel of your space.

Above Dark slate-coloured slabs and pale gravel make an attractive contrast for paths and patios.
Below left The apparently random arrangement of different-sized setts adds to the organic feel of this path.
Below right This gently curving path is designed to make the garden feel bigger – and kids (and big kids) can hop down it if they like!

PRIVACY AND SCREENING

When starting work on your garden, it may seem that the simplest solution is to rip everything out and start from scratch. The plain canvas has so much appeal: we all want to make our mark, stamp a personal identity on our piece of the urban jungle. But maybe others have been there before us and their planting remains. What do we do? We might not like the way the garden has been planted by the previous owners, but there could be some gems in there, well worth including in your own plans. This applies in particular to mature trees and shrubs. Don't be in too much of a hurry to get rid of these as they could be a great asset, acting as screening or camouflage and creating instant privacy. Once you take them out, the garden will look stark and immature.

First, the trees. If you have mature trees in the garden, especially on your boundaries, you're lucky, since trees take forever to reach a good size (except, of course, for the dreaded Leyland cypress). And if you are blessed with other mature trees, especially fruit trees (apples, pears, plums, mulberries) or decorative trees (flowering cherries, flowering crabs and maples), you'd be daft to fell them, unless they're diseased. Ask yourself why that tree was planted where it is. What did the previous owners want to conceal? Maybe it hides an eyesore which won't be revealed fully until you cut the tree down; or it may stop your neighbours from looking right in at you – or vice versa. To cut down a mature tree takes minutes. To realise you've made a mistake will cost you years and years of waiting for a tiny sapling to bulk up. In the meantime, whatever you wanted to screen will be staring at you for a long, long time!

There is a narrow line between a tree that provides natural screening and a tree which casts too much shade. But rather than remove a shady tree altogether, have the tree's canopy 'lifted' by a professional tree surgeon. This involves removing some of the lower branches, and thinning out the others. It's definitely a job for a trained professional – amateur thinning produces some of the worst horticultural disasters I've ever seen! If you have a tree or large shrub that's too dominant, think of turning it into a standard; you'll still have some canopy higher up, where it's useful for screening, but lower down the bulk will be reduced. I urge you to keep trees at all costs – the urban environment needs them.

Evergreen shrubs, especially those which have scented flowers and/or winter colour, will be the mainstay of the winter garden, so think twice about getting rid of them. You will often find that where mature planting is casting too much shade, just taking out one of the trees or shrubs will allow in plenty of light, without compromising an effective screen, and the rest of the planting will benefit from the additional elbow room.

If a shrub is in the wrong place, but could be used for screening elsewhere, wait until winter and then move it. Even mature shrubs can be moved quite happily as long as you dig up the largest possible rootball, minimise disturbance to the roots, and water it regularly once it is transplanted to its new position (especially in summer, when it might need drenching every other day). If it dies, you're no worse off, and at least you've got rid of the original problem. And if it survives, clever you!

Left Unlike most other gum trees, *Eucalyptus niphophila* will not overpower a small urban garden, taking ten years to grow to a height of only 8m/25ft.

Below With its sweet pea-like flowers, heart-shaped leaves and slow growth, and despite its common name – Judas tree – *Cercis siliquastrum* is heavenly for an urban garden.

TREES FOR SMALL CITY GARDENS

Evergreen trees include:

Trachycarpus fortunei (chusan palm), with large fan-shaped leaves it's an ideal focal point, but it needs a warm site protected from wind and frost to thrive.

Eucalyptus niphophila (snow gum), a slow grower compared to other sweet gums, this eucalyptus has lovely green, cream and grey dappled bark contrasting with thick, leathery, grey-green leaves.

Ceanothus arboreus is a tree species of the Californian lilac, but will only grow to a height of 6m/20ft. Like many of the most popular shrub varieties, such as *C. 'Burkwoodii'*, it produces brilliant blue flowers in spring but needs a sunny position to thrive.

Deciduous trees include:

Cercis siliquastrum (Judas tree), which produces pink or white sweet pea-like flowers on the bare branches before the leaves open. A graceful spreader that gives dappled shade beneath its branches, providing ideal conditions for planting underneath.

Sorbus cashmiriana (Kashmir rowan), with soft grey-green leaves and pale pink flowers, followed by berries which last into winter.

Betula pendula (silver birch) will grow fast, but won't dominate or cast heavy shade; a trio will screen quite well and, being native, support a host of wildlife.

ADDING TREES

If your garden is practically bare of trees or large shrubs, try to add one or two, siting them carefully. Trees have a real presence and contribute so much to the urban garden. They are living green screens, shielding you from neighbours and ugly eyesores, and they provide sheltered seating areas, hideaways for kids and adults, leafy canopies under which to chill out in dappled shade, as well as windbreaks to soften high-rise gusts. And if you pick the right ones you can have scented flowers, edible fruit or berries, autumn leaf colour, the texture of winter bark and/or shapely skeletons, as well as delicate new leaf colour in spring. No wonder I like them so much!

While evergreens provide year-round screening, deciduous screening in winter will reveal only too well the eyesore it hides so effectively in summer. Remember the idea of perspective, too: if you have an ugly building on your garden boundary, then by all means plant a sapling close up against it as a long-term solution, but while it is growing large enough for camouflage, plant something closer to your viewpoint for the short term so that, from where you sit and look out on the garden, the eyesore is blocked from your sight-line. The butterfly bush (*Buddleja davidii*) is a wonderfully fast growing shrub, shooting up several feet a year while relatively young, so is ideal for new gardens. It's not another Leyland cypress, however, seldom reaching more than 5m/16ft eventually, but it screens well in summer and has scented flowers which attract masses of butterflies.

OTHER SOLUTIONS

If you don't have large shrubs or trees or can't wait for the saplings you have planted to bulk up to maturity (and can't afford to buy in mature specimens), there are other ways of providing effective screening and privacy. The way you do this will depend on what you are screening out and whether you are overlooked from the back, the sides or above.

Where you have the option, always go for living screening. This might take the form of a narrow 'fedge' (is it a hedge, or is it a fence?!) of living bamboo or willow. It will move in the breeze, arch gracefully, change with the seasons and last practically forever. It will need little maintenance, apart from light pruning or, in the case of bamboo, mowing round the edges to cut off any new shoots which threaten to make the fedge thicker than you wish. Fedges are fun and trendy and not many people have them – yet they work wonderfully well.

Another form of living screen is a framework smothered with a climber. Any openwork support is useful to the urban gardener when it comes to creating private areas, as it looks great by itself, but even better when covered by a climbing plant which will blur the structure's linear character. Wooden trellis is the most obvious framework to clothe with a plant, but iron latticework, tautly strung ropes, and nylon netting or wire tensioned between vine eyes, also do the job well. Once the screening plant is established, you won't even see the supporting framework.

This type of screen is equally good at partitioning off your private space in the garden as it is at hiding the compost bins or camouflaging the shed. The main considerations are that the supporting framework is sturdy enough to hold the climber when mature, and that the structure to which the framework is attached is strong enough to support the whole caboodle, even in a gale or when covered in snow. There is one other obvious consideration: will the screening still look graceful

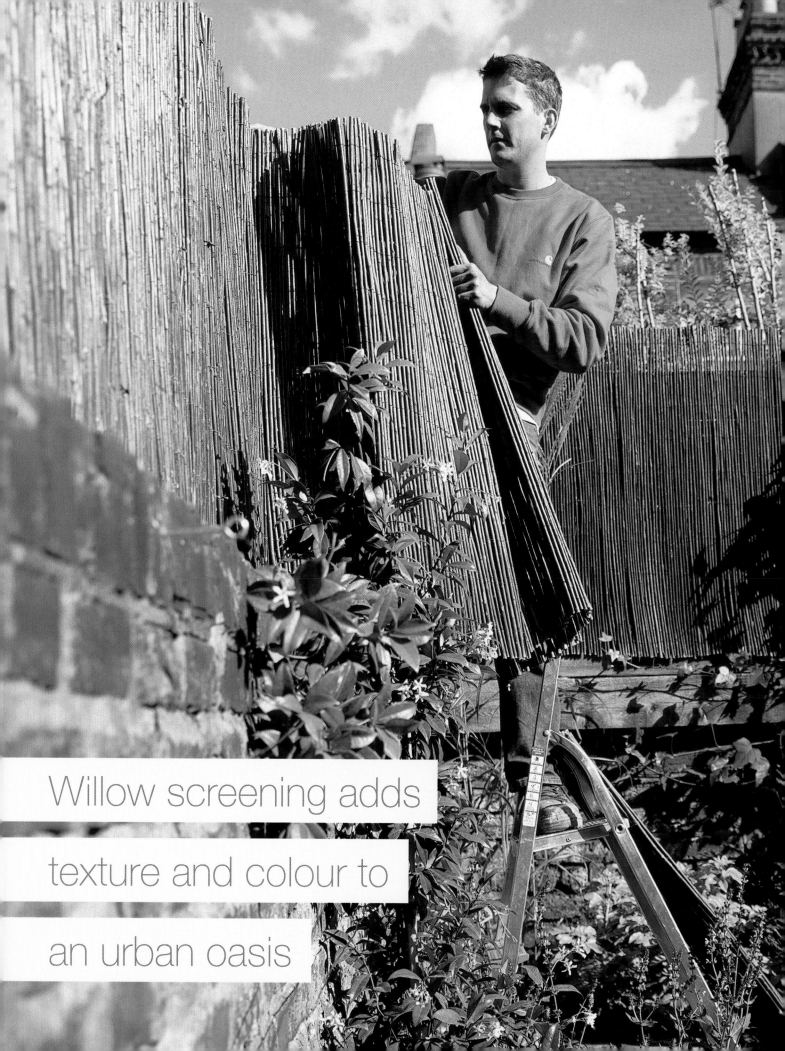

Willow screening adds texture and colour to an urban oasis

and effective when winter comes and most plants lose their leaves? Thankfully, most trelliswork is an architectural feature all by itself.

To create privacy from above, you can easily make covered areas by slatting horizontal beams across a vertical framework and allowing rampant climbers to work their way across. *Clematis montana* 'Elizabeth' is a vigorous climber with masses of nutmeg-scented flowers in spring: it will cover practically anything, happily galloping over that ugly shed, growing through a sturdy tree, or quickly covering a trellised or slatted roof structure. Plants like this allow light to filter through, while providing excellent screening from above, and also give seasonal displays of colourful scented flowers. *Clematis armandii* 'Apple Blossom' is another vigorous climber with scented flowers in early spring, yet it is evergreen as well, though it does best in a sheltered, protected site. And how about this for a bit of casual one-upmanship? Grow your own grapes! Make your own wine! Vines are excellent at covering an overhead screen and they are not difficult to grow: you can casually pick grapes while basking in the late summer sun ('Boskoop Glory' for dessert grapes, 'Siegerrebe' for wine making, both suited to southerly English climes). More traditional choices are fragrant roses and jasmine for sunny spots, or honeysuckle (*Lonicera*) and trachelospermum for the shadier positions.

If you have problems with wind, the best type of shelter is provided by evergreen trees: the strawberry tree (*Arbutus unedo*), hollies (*Ilex*), Portuguese laurel (*Prunus lusitanica*), the Lawson cypress (*Chamaecyparis lawsoniana*) and yew (*Taxus*). But you can also effectively use well-anchored trellis, latticework or board-on-board fencing. Solid obstacles, like walls or solid fences, just cause the wind to come roaring over, whereas permeable barriers filter and mollify it.

Creating privacy, and screening yourself from eyesores or prying eyes, can be a test of your creativity. Let your imagination run riot: from canvas sails stretched over an enclosed courtyard, creating an exotic Berber-style dining area gently shaded from the fierce midday sun, to shady green hideaways, tucked out of sight among huge foliage plants like palms, tree ferns and bamboos. It's your space – play with it!

DEFINING YOUR SPACE

If your garden is just one flat area with no change of level, the space may look one-dimensional unless it is bursting with plants – more interest is needed. Features which create a change of level define the space and provide the eye with satisfying lines and textural components. They help to give a garden character and the functional elements within it an identity. For example, a raised patio works well as an area for sitting out, but also adds a height dimension to the garden, offering new perspectives. Defining space is really a question of working out what you want the space to be used for, then deciding on tangible ways to make this happen.

A simple path from one end of the garden to the other is one way of defining space, dividing the overall area into sections and leading on to others. But when is a path not just a path? It could take on all the excitement of a mystery journey at night – especially if it weaves and curves and you can't see where it's going. Lighting the way with candles at intervals leads the stroller to – what? – a secret meeting on the bench under the honeysuckle? A quiet drink, alone? Who knows! The path has moved from being a functional element to a piece of hard landscaping that leads you on a journey.

Perhaps you have already decided where you want to grow your plants by marking off an area which you have designated as 'border'. A way of defining that further, and making a desirable feature at the same time, would be to construct raised beds. These can be edged with wooden planks, metal strips, railway sleepers, logs, bricks or stone.

Below Combining a seating area with a pergola allows you to grow climbers for shade on hot summer days.

Because you've given the ordinary a lift, the border immediately becomes something special, even before it's been planted up.

You might, in turn, decide that you want another area specifically for entertaining. You would choose the materials and construct the area to suit that purpose. Certain structures, like the pergola, define space horizontally and vertically. They invite you to gravitate to it, to walk slowly through it, to sit under its almost absent cover. Pergolas are clever illusions: they contain the space so loosely, with their uprights and horizontal timbers so far apart, yet the effect is to make us feel that the space beneath has a totally different atmosphere. Pergolas can be any size you please; garden centres and DIY stores sell kits, or you can buy the timber from a timber yard and make your own. They don't necessarily have to be rectangular either. Even the smallest garden might have room for a pergola, although if your garden is very shady you might wish to let it remain unclothed, without climbers running across the timbers. It will still feel special.

MAKING USE OF LEVELS

On a sloping garden, brick or stone terracing makes the space more manageable and opens up all sorts of interesting possibilities for planting. Terracing involves a set of retaining walls, each holding back a considerable weight of soil. These have to be properly made, with footings to support the brickwork above. You can use thick timbers, such as railway sleepers, but these have to be fastened securely. Good drainage is also essential in the building of terraces, otherwise you may find yourself staring at a descending series of ponds!

Terracing involves far more work than laying a patio, even though the result of all your labouring cannot obviously be seen, since it lies underground in the foundations. However, your visual reward comes from all the gorgeous plants that will thrive in the deep, level beds and which you otherwise wouldn't have been able to grow. If your garden has a steep incline and you would like to terrace it, get quotes from builders who specialise in this kind of work; leave the headache to them!

Below left With raised beds the elements of a garden work on several levels, opening out an enclosed space.
Below Even on a small scale, incorporating levels into a design adds interest.

Above Decking is a bit of a magician: it can impose order on the garden while seeming to allow the plants free rein!

DECKING

At ground level, spaces can be further defined by the choice of materials: a lawn for the kids to play on, or a brick area with pots full of herbs for morning coffee. One of the more dramatic ways to do this is with decking. Now, people are talking about decking these days as if it's an out-dated cliché. Just because decking has received a lot of exposure on television doesn't mean that it's not great for your garden – some things are popular simply because they're good! As you can probably guess, I'm a great fan of the stuff. It is a natural material, tough, versatile and can be laid in all manner of shapes, while its textural appearance immediately makes a statement and works well with plants. It doesn't need anything else done to it to make it more pretty: an expanse of bare decking overhanging a pond, for example, will look so right you won't want to clutter it up.

Decking is a natural material yet also trendy, and seems to have been designed specially for the urban garden, whereas in a huge country garden it can look out of place. Decking can be used in super-creative ways. You can play with levels, having two or three huge decking 'steps' leading off from one another, at any angle you fancy. It always looks neat, modern and is a great place to

sit, to display your geraniums and for the kids to play. It invites you to look at the pleasing surface and enjoy the relaxed neatness in its construction.

You don't have to put a deck next to the house; you can use decking free-form throughout the garden, where it can mimic other shapes or lead you from one area to the next. You can tuck half of it into a planting scheme so that one end appears to emerge from lush green foliage. You can daringly extend it out over a pond and watch the cat sit there mesmerised all day long! And if you have a sloping garden, rejoice: decking equals laziness and you can simply build a deck over the slope. If the slope is steep, the area underneath can be planted up or you can make it into a den for the kids. And making a deck is within the DIY grasp of the average person – except for very steep slopes when you might need the advice of a professional.

Decks can be made in either softwood or hardwood. Softwood is cheaper, but hardwood lasts longer. It comes in planks or ready-made squares, and you have a choice as to the colour of the wood and the grain. Some decking materials are ridged to improve grip in wet weather. I should mention here that it's only advisable to site decking in areas that get sun because in perpetual shade it can become slimy and slippery.

OTHER SPACE-DEFINING FEATURES

Since they occupy an area, garden sculptures define space and, as such, have to be carefully sited. Often you won't know exactly where a sculpture is going to look best until you get it in place – and then decide it'll look better somewhere else! Sculptural features used in repetition, such as a row of painted timber obelisks in a border or a row of box topiary lining a path, bring atmosphere to an area. These formal elements can add an air of gentle solemnity or even comedy to parts of the garden which don't have much else happening, or they can act as scene stealers in their own right. Hedging can be used to create a sense of enclosure. Even a low box hedge says something about the space it surrounds, giving a tiny vertical lift to whatever's behind it.

On a roof terrace the planters will provide changes of level. You could have a series of hidden steps to raise pots above each other, thus creating a wall of foliage and flowers. Defining the space there might mean temporary structures in summer, marking off sections of the garden, such as a canopy near the house.

Light also defines spaces. The clever use of uplighters among trees and shrubs, or downlighters on a path, will help you enjoy the garden for more hours of the day. The purple-red trunks of *Prunus serrula*, for example, will seem to glow in the dark with a bit of clever lighting! Spot lighting pinpoints one object but throws heavy mysterious shadows around it, while ambient wall lights glow after dark, their mood peaceful. Using uplighters in water is very dramatic, but shining lights on water cascading down a wall is better than TV!

A PLACE TO ENTERTAIN

Eating and entertaining space is one of the most important components of your garden. If there isn't room for a separate kids' play space, why not think of a built-in seating area as multi-functional – somewhere the kids will play during the day, and a place for you to take over in the evening for eating, drinking and entertaining? You'll probably spend a lot of time in this particular area, so allocate a decent amount of space to it. Make sure it will take a table and as many chairs as you're likely to need. Make room, too, for pots and tubs to frame your seating area, and fill these with plants of brilliant colour and scent to enhance the mood.

Don't begin any construction until you've carefully marked out on the ground the proposed dimensions of your seating area. It may fit on

paper, but will you be able to squeeze past everybody's knees when it's a reality? Allow plenty of room for chairs to be pulled back and arranged in a relaxed manner. You need room to stretch out here – that's what the space is being designed for. Imagine trying to get a tray-load of drinks onto the table past your guests: if it feels like an obstacle course, or only negotiable if you balance the tray on your head, you'll need to think again!

If your garden is really tiny, it will be hard to incorporate a completely separate entertaining space. Instead, pave the whole area to make it look bigger. This mimics a courtyard, and you can devote whatever space you like to the paraphernalia of entertaining. A simple bistro table on the sunniest side, perhaps, or locating the whole lot in the centre of the space – the choice is yours. It's easy to add plants and greenery with judicious use of pots and planters and nothing looks more inviting than a garden area which just begs you to eat and enjoy yourselves outdoors.

Another idea which works well in small gardens is sinking your seating area into the ground. Sunken spaces are exciting, add a touch of the dramatic and create atmosphere, all at once. We all love surprises, and the garden is a wonderful place in which to have them. A sunken area smugly screams 'design', and will become a real conversation piece that all your friends want to emulate. First dig out a pit, making sure it's deep and wide enough to fit in a table and chairs with

plenty of room for lounging. Then put a thin layer of hardcore and gravel in the bottom for drainage; you'll need more serious drainage if you live over a clay subsoil. Border the sides with simple breeze-block walls to retain the soil, then paint or render them. Top it all off with some attractive pressure-treated timber so the sides are comfortable to sit on. You're down among the plants, looking up on the world!

Raised seating areas constructed from timber decking are well suited to outdoor entertaining as they're functional and beautiful and can be used all year round. I know I've already waxed lyrical about the benefits of decking, but it really is a material perfectly suited to a social space. It will tolerate everything from stiletto heels to wheelchairs and is therefore ideal if you have to think about ease of access and durability.

If you have a choice, remember to site your seating area in the sun and away from trees, so that leaves and berries don't make the surface slippery or, far worse, drop into your pina colada! Make sure it's also within easy reach of the house, especially if you're planning to carry out the roast dinner with all the trimmings!

If you want a barbecue, avoid one that's built-in. They take up too much space in a small garden and you can't move them if the wind changes direction and forces smoke into the house or onto your guests. And what happens when it starts to rain? A fixed barbecue is dead space when you're not using it, which is for at least seven months of the year in our climate. There are numerous portable models available, in various shapes and sizes, most of which can be folded up and stored out of the way when not required.

If you have room for a separate play area, ensure that your seating space is protected from footballs, frisbees and the like. Use a trellis barrier and plant it up with tough climbers like clematis or ivy. Then surround your seating area with fragrant plants and be soothed by privacy and scent as the footballs fly! Evergreen *Pittosporum tobira*, or its silver-and-green variegated version, would be ideal, as would wintersweet (*Chimonanthus praecox*) – my mum's favourite plant because of its sweet-smelling yellow flowers which appear in the depths of winter. The toughie *Abeliophyllum distichum*, a relative of forsythia but far less vigorous, is my personal favourite. Its fragrant white pink-tinged flowers which appear in early spring are absolutely gorgeous. These shrubs are drought tolerant and need full sun, but hopefully that's probably where you'll site your seating area. Alternatively you could surround your seating with willow fencing, rose-smothered trellis, or 50cm/20in-wide rills of still, reflective water. That should do the trick!

GARDEN FURNITURE

The recent gardening boom has seen an enormous range of outdoor furniture readily available on the high street. No more plastic roadside picnic tables – today we're much more style conscious! You can buy garden seating in many different materials including plastic, wood, metal, glass and natural stone. Wooden furniture made of pine, mahogany, teak or cedar is by far the most popular. Comfortable, it will suit most garden styles, especially when you tart it up with an appropriate cushion. An oiling every couple of years is all that's needed to stop it deteriorating.

Natural stone is a lovely material, even for seating, but it does need cushions as it's a cold surface. But stone is expensive, and due to its weight is not a good idea for a balcony or roof terrace – whereas plastic furniture is ideal for such gardens. Now, did I say that? Mention plastic furniture and everybody winces. But plastic outdoor furniture has come a long way since the 1960s and 1970s. Nowadays designers like Ron Arid and Philippe Starck have given a modern twist to plastic furniture, designing outdoor seating that is well suited to contemporary gardens.

Elegant wrought iron seats are best for period gardens, as are wicker and woven willow furniture, while ornate benches in iron or teak will add an air of formality. Or you could get hold of a large log, place it in a shady corner and, once it's covered with moss, it'll shout bucolic bliss. Reclamation

yards are good hunting grounds for unusual seating, too. You don't need to spend a fortune to have a functional, attractive bench. Don't sacrifice comfort for aesthetic appeal – a seat may look good but it also has to be comfortable to sit on.

Above Plant *Chimonanthus praecox* and in the dark depths of winter you'll be treated to a beautiful display of yellow flowers just laden with scent.

CREATING TRANQUILLITY

Our busy urban lifestyles revolve around work, speed and entertainment. People often complain that they're bored when they stop doing anything because we are a nation of stimulation seekers. Yet, in tandem with this, we also recognise that we want gardens to be places where the opposite happens: where there isn't much going on, where our weary eyes can rest, where there's nothing loud, dramatic or exciting to pump up the adrenalin – where we can feel at peace. In short, we crave peace and tranquillity in our back yards.

How do you create tranquillity in a city garden? It might be an easy task in the country where the traffic and the noise are not an issue, but surely, in a densely packed, frantic urban environment, it's well-nigh impossible to find a peaceful oasis?

THE JAPANESE EXAMPLE

Creating tranquillity is an art perfected by the Japanese and many have looked to them for inspiration. Their gardens exemplify some of the most relaxing and spiritually nourishing places in the world. And most of them are in the very heart of the city! These gardens are models of understatement, quite different in character to our western gardens. Here, we often think more is better, cramming in as many plants as we can, but the essence of the Japanese garden is the opposite: restraint. But you don't need a minimalist planting scheme or a raked gravel area to give you the ultimate chill-out zone, although you can learn a lot from books on Japanese gardening.

The Japanese design their gardens as places to experience solitude and contemplation, rather than for entertainment or recreation. Nothing is random, neither the planting, nor the positioning of stones, even though it may appear so. There are few flowers but what flowers there are get real appreciation – the Japanese take time off work to see the cherry blossom in spring, and have special picnics called *hanami* in honour of the flowers! Japan is a wet country, so green predominates. Ferns and bamboo are everywhere, and moss covers stones and ground alike, like a carpet. Water is a dominant feature, with ponds, streams and waterfalls in all the best gardens. If there is no water, the Japanese symbolise it with gravel and slates made to look like rivers.

I mention Japanese gardening in particular because it seems to exemplify what tranquil spaces are all about, not so that you immediately rush out and go oriental! Creating a Japanese garden in your own back yard might seem easy enough – after all, these are minimalist spaces, you might think. But it's not as easy as it might first appear. For one thing, the Japanese view their gardens as intensely spiritual places, deeply bound up with their culture. They simply garden in a different way to us. But their way of evoking tranquillity outdoors has many principles we can learn and apply to our own gardens. I remember seeing this carried out on a tiny London balcony, too small for the owner to even walk out onto. He had spread the minute floor area with pale grey gravel, raked it into a pattern and added a single rush in a pot, plus a stone Buddha. It looked superb! So I urge you to read about the Japanese gardeners and absorb their philosophy before tackling your own space.

SEEKING INSPIRATION

We've all been to places in the countryside, and visited gardens that seem to invite peaceful reflection and make us feel we could chill out there for hours. Try to work out what creates this relaxing ambience – what features do these places share? We can translate some of them to our small spaces, as well as adding a few others to help our specific urban problems.

Look to your senses. We experience positive relaxing feelings through what we see and hear, especially. We can do much to create visually tranquil gardens that provoke an instant feel-good reaction, and, by the introduction of moving water and small sounds within the space, amplify that feeling still further. When I think about what might

Above One way to achieve a peaceful atmosphere is to position a seating area right in among the plants.
Far left Classic Japanese planting – such as irises and miniature maples – does make use of colour, but in a restrained manner.
Left Gazebo-type covered seating creates instant seclusion, and there's also the option to grow climbers over it for greater privacy.

make a garden tranquil, I think of silence, stillness, lots of green, pastel flowers, shade, dappled sunlight, seclusion. I also think of water: still ponds with koi flashing their brilliant orange and red colours just under the surface, caught in a ray of sunlight. I see curves rather than angles. I see neatness, but not of the obsessive kind, and I see different textures and shapes. I see enclosed, contained space – not a meadow, however beautiful that is.

Hard day? A garden is the place to retreat and chill out

I might also notice the planting. In a Japanese garden this might be dozens of clipped flat-topped azaleas with nothing underneath them except the same kind of moss or fern. So, lots of plants of one type, and repetition of a certain form. This is not boring, rather it soothes, allowing us to come back down to earth after a busy day, in a green, visually undemanding cocoon. Shady gardeners should celebrate! Nothing creates a peaceful atmosphere better than pools of shade.

It's also helpful to think of things that are the opposite to these tranquil spaces. I'm reminded instantly of amenity planting schemes which shout loud with scarlets, purples, lime greens and other primaries, summer bedding in regimented rows, in beds that have no other planting around them to relate to. Some planting schemes are like the visual representation of a migraine headache. There's nothing sympathetic in this way of planting, it's functional and bright and it lasts – but only for a season. It's no accident that many of us do not copy municipal plantings throughout our entire garden. They have no permanence and, somehow, we know it. Having too many different species planted cheek by jowl may look colourful, but the effect can be hectic. The eye roves about the design restlessly and cannot relax, simply because there's too much going on.

Brilliant sunshine is not tranquil either. You may relax in its warmth, but its brightness gets too much after a time, while dappled shade invites us to enter and escape the heat. A garden to meander in is equivalent to the winding down of a hurried mind. It's like a walking meditation, the eye moving in an unhurried way from one feature to the next, with nothing dazzling or dramatic along the way. Everything flows and blends.

NATURAL MATERIALS

Natural materials make the space feel as though it has its roots in the calming, solid presence of the earth. If you have a concrete patio, for example, replacing it with a softly coloured natural stone will change the atmosphere immediately. Gardens with a lot of concrete features, or dominant concrete features, are not calming, rather they enervate. Perhaps they subconsciously remind us of the workaday world from which we long to escape! If you do like concrete, you'll need to soften it considerably with lots of plants.

Natural materials have irregularities which contribute to a peaceful ambience, whereas concrete or reconstituted paving stones just don't feel as though they have been around for long. In the same vein, old railway sleepers look great as steps, as inserts into brick and gravel areas, and as the sides to raised beds. If you make a pergola, explore how you might make it from rustic

Left Solid yet softened with age, railway sleepers are perfect for raised beds.
Below left Roses scrambling over an arch is a classic feature of cottage garden design, but there's nothing to stop you recreating it in an urban setting.

Right Bamboos – here, a golden *Phyllostachys* – are vigorous enough growers to plant for hedges. And no privet hedge will make such a soothing sound in a breeze!
Below The scent of lavender is used in aromatherapy – so why not harness its soothing properties in your garden?
Far right Many azaleas have a compact and bushy growth, ideal for small gardens, and there are so many different colourful hybrids out there.

materials, or select wood for the framework that doesn't have a brand new, squared-off look. Decking looks fabulous and over the years the wood mellows to an attractive silver-grey finish.

But not all artificial or man-made materials are unsuitable – it depends on how they are used. Stainless steel and shiny metals might seem so hard and unforgiving that they would be the antithesis of calm. But their nature is to reflect and, like water (where their use is often complementary), they give out rather than take. If you use modern materials, explore nearby planting carefully – an abundance of grasses, or mossy looking plants in rounded shapes, works well.

PLANTS AND FEATURES

Certain plants evoke calm. Bamboos have timeless properties, yet they're trendy enough for a modern urban garden. Lavenders with their soft grey leaves and subtle scent have a still, soothing quality. While a rose arch, with the fragrant creamy white blossoms of *Rosa* 'Mme Alfred Carrière' tumbling down, takes us back a step in time. Plants with big leaves, like hostas, are solid, dependable and quiet, while ferns exude the still, sanctuary-like atmosphere of the grotto. Herbs, grown together in a group, have a gentle, soothing character and trailing plants, like ivies, suggest relaxed informality. Ferns and mosses are *de rigueur*, as are those mounded or rounded shapes, like box balls and prostate junipers, azaleas or *Lonicera nitida*. Of course, anything spiky is out! Yucca, often used as an architectural plant, has no place in a tranquil garden as its spines have a real feral bite! If you need a vertical accent in a container or a border, there are kinder plants to be found.

Above left Creating a water feature from an old cast-iron pump will bring a rustic influence to a garden.
Above right If our great-grandparents could see their mangle used as a pot stand – they'd probably rejoice!
Left With the lush, deep-green foliage of the clematis all around, sitting in this gazebo feels as if you're in a forest arbour.

Above Highly formal garden designs need not feel sterile and uninviting – here, still water and cottage-style planting soften the effect.

Above top When planning a water feature try to marry it in with the planting, otherwise it can look stark and isolated.

Above right The sound of water flowing over pebbles helps to block out city distractions, concentrating the mind on just chilling out.

Old objects, such as large stones and rocks, or old-fashioned household implements from junk yards, engender a peaceful feeling in the garden. The Japanese use these a lot, lifting great boulders into place beside streams to give an age-old feel, that important sense of permanence. You might be able to get hold of an old millstone or an old cast-iron water pump from a reclamation yard, features which will add to the ambience. Water and peaceful gardens also go well together. Create a secret pond whose edges seem to fade away into soothing green planting around it – even if you're using a rubber pond liner.

Noise is a big problem in the city, and one of the enemies of peace. Some noises you can't control. You can't do much about the traffic, or about children shrieking next door – though this noise is probably only temporary. But you can distract. When the wind blows, a large clump of bamboo will make a sound like the rustling of paper skirts – quite noticeable and unusual. Another excellent idea is to install a water feature, and I've included a special section on using water

in a garden on pages 80–81. These are very effective at grabbing the attention and making the ambient noise level around you fade away.

Lighting up the garden at night creates a wonderful peaceful ambience. Have a row of tiny tea-lights in jars at the edge of a pathway leading to a pond, running them all the way round it. On a warm August evening the atmosphere will be quite magical and meditative.

If you have a sunny garden and you want a tranquil spot, you'll have to block out the hot summer sun with a canopy overhead, or a pergola overhung with climbers. The ideal is to make a tucked-away area, a private, well-cared for space that feels nurturing, inviting you to sit and contemplate. And despite the paradox of living in the city, we can create little back yards which fulfil the need for tranquil spaces just as effectively as a walk in the country. We can turn the city environment to our advantage and make it work for us, simply because city gardens have that all-important quality of being enclosed, like a contained outdoor room.

WATER

Try to represent all the elements – air, fire, earth and water – in your garden to bring a sense of balance and harmony. Water is very easily incorporated, so think of ingenious ways to introduce it into your outdoor living space so that you can enjoy its soothing effects.

Water is life, movement, vitality. It deserves a place in every garden, no matter how small. It refreshes the air, cools it in summer (think of the Trevi fountains in Rome), and grounds pollution. The sound of playing fountains masks noise and their presence provides a focal point, which is great if you need to draw attention into the heart of the garden because of a dominant eyesore outside its boundaries. Fountains also play with light and reflect it in charming ways.

In a city garden you don't need a simply amazing water feature complete with huge pumps, waterfalls and the like. Water features can be tiny. A small fish-tank pump no longer than your little finger can be used in a 35cm/14in pot to give an audible bubbling jet above a pile of artistically arranged stones and pieces of driftwood. This would be suitable even for a tiny high-rise balcony or among the planters on a roof terrace.

Ponds need full sun. If you site them in the shade they can turn disgustingly rank. Position them well away from trees too: leaves foul up the water and upset the pond's balance. You can have a wildlife pond which lets nature gradually take over (see page 26), or a filtered mini-ocean for precious koi. And a pond can be any size, from a half-barrel with a dwarf water lily and a couple of fish, to one several metres across, complete with bridges and decks! Wildlife will be drawn into the garden, as will human observers, because water attracts all life.

I urge you to think seriously about having moving water in one form or another in your garden space. To hear the sound of water moving, even if it's just from a small bubble fountain hidden under pebbles, is very peaceful indeed. For shady areas, choose a wall-mounted spout. A lion's head looks particularly dramatic pouring water into a shallow stone basin beneath, partly hidden by the foliage of ferns or a fatsia. If you have young children, forego the pond proper until they are much older, unless you fix a metal grid over the surface. Instead, go for the charm of a bubble fountain partially hidden among hostas; with bubble fountains there's no water to fall into.

In making a garden pond you can either use a pre-formed rigid liner or a flexible liner, preferably made of butyl rubber. These will adapt to any irregularities in the shape of the hole, but you do have to conceal the edges carefully, with stones, grass or plants. You could place coloured glass chips at the bottom of a modern pool, or clear glass marbles which sparkle like diamonds when the sun shines.

Planting the surrounding area should present no problems as long as you use plants sympathetic to the waterside. This means creating a boggy area especially for them. You can't just plant water lovers in ordinary soil on the other side of your pond liner and expect them to flourish! You need to extend the liner, burying it under the earth, so that it will keep the soil there continually moist for the bog plants to grow in.

Make use of water's reflective qualities. Remember that what you plant nearby will be doubled in a still pool, so choose something architectural. And build in lighting for night-time drama by uplighting waterfalls and ponds, creating a surreal effect.

1: *Iris germanica*
2: Water meadow garden
3: *Nymphaea* 'Attraction'
4: *Astilbe* 'Venus'
5: *Nymphaea* 'Mme Wilfon Gonnère'

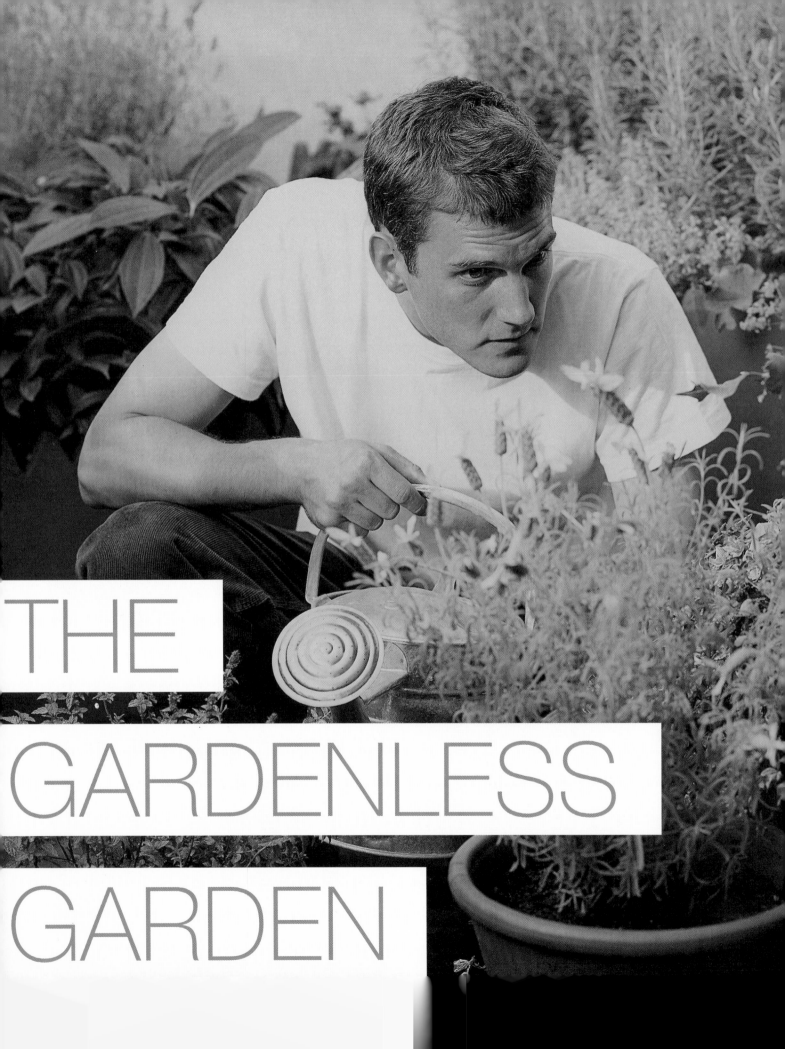

THE
GARDENLESS
GARDEN

One of my mates lives on a houseboat on the Thames, but you should see what he grows on his floating home – it's a great example of what I mean by a gardenless garden. You don't need to step off dry land, though, to see what inventive gardeners have conjured into creation despite lacking that apparent essential – a piece of ground. Just look up! Some of the loveliest floral displays belong to people who live storeys-high in tower blocks and cultivate window boxes overflowing with trailing geraniums and blue lobelias, herbs and tiny conifers. Other people are just as imaginative with their roof patios, balconies and postage stamp-sized concrete backyards. Such gardenless gardeners brighten up the city for the rest of us and deserve our thanks and admiration. They've discovered you don't need that piece of ground: given a flowerpot, hanging basket or other suitable container, compost, water and nutrients, plants will romp away.

Below Gardens can come in many shapes, sizes and guises. Don't let the absence of ground space deter you.

They've discovered something else, too – that containers are liberating; they put you in control, and give you confidence. Making a success of containers is far easier than tackling an entire garden, so they can be a great way for the novice gardener to gain experience. What's more, because you're not dictated to by the local soil conditions, you can grow plants not typically associated with your area. And because containers can be rearranged at any time, and replanted as soon as one season's show ends, you can make your gardenless garden a revolving stage set.

CONTAIN YOURSELF!

Plants in containers are like pets: you can fall under the spell of their instant appeal, then discover that they demand time and commitment. With something so satisfying and easy, there have to be a few spanners in the works. That's life, I guess! Before you go out and buy your containers, and long before you consider the care of the plants growing in them, there are just a few practical considerations you need to think about before getting really stuck in: where to safely put them, what the conditions are like, how to protect them from wind, and how best to ensure the ravenous little beasts are kept fed and watered.

WEIGH UP THE OPTIONS

If you're creating a gardenless garden on a roof or balcony, don't assume that the building's construction will take the weight of heavy containers. Let's say you have a roof terrace. You can't plonk a load of heavy concrete and terracotta containers straight down the middle, or the roof will cave in! Your garden will then become the main talking point of the neighbourhood, but for all the wrong reasons... Terraces and balconies have a specific load-bearing capacity, and you need to identify this before you start. Containers are often very heavy when full of soil and saturated with water. A reliable roofing contractor or a structural engineer should be able to advise you on how much weight a roof or balcony will safely take.

You may also need to find out where the main supports are: these will bear the weight of heavy containers more reliably than the intervening spans. If you can't obtain such expert advice, play safe and opt for plastic or glass-fibre containers. Okay, these might not be the classiest looking objects, but they weigh far less than the alternatives. You can always conceal them behind just one or two terracotta or stone pots. Or if you grow creeping plants like nasturtiums, they'll quickly spill out and cover the sides.

OVER EXPOSED

Roof and balcony gardeners know only too well that their number-one problem is exposure. In windy weather, tall plants may blow over and get damaged, and if they're planted in terracotta containers, the pots can get smashed as well! You can grow tall plants in containers but it might be necessary to have a system for anchoring them to the wall.

If you have an ugly view that you want to screen out with climbing plants growing up a support – such as Boston ivy (*Parthenocissus tricuspidata*) on a trellis – make sure the support is fixed to something solid, or the whole thing might take off like a sail! Additionally, make sure all your pots and containers are well anchored – or they could fall off and maybe injure a passerby. Well-secured bamboo and reed screens could also be used to create a windstill environment, while looking very attractive in the right situation. Alternatively, artificial screens made from UV-resistant plastics will provide protection from strong winds. Most are bespoke, however, and as a result can work out expensive. If you do go for plastics, make sure they are at least 50% permeable – a slight breeze is essential to blow off dirt and grime and help prevent pests and diseases.

Right Grasses, aucuba and lavender are all tough plants that will continue to thrive in a windy location.

Below left Dramatic spiky Agaves make a bold contrast with delicate, bright, white daisies and a soft cascade of Convolvulus.

Below right Tiers of window boxes crowd the sills above a narrow city street, relieving this brick canyon with their masses of colourful blooms.

Far left Water containers in the evening when the day is cooling down. Otherwise, the water evaporates before reaching the roots – and direct sun on wet foliage can cause scorching.
Left Simple devices like these dippers help to conserve water and make sure it reaches the parts where it is needed – and they also save time.

QUENCH THEIR THIRST

Container-grown plants are dependent beasts, looking entirely to you, their carer, for feeding and watering. You can't leave a planted-up pot to take its chance, especially in summer. This might be a problem if you are out all day or go off on holiday for a fortnight and don't have anyone who could pop in and water your plants. It's not like you can send them off to the plant equivalent of a kennels (though I'm sure there's a money-making opportunity in that idea for some would-be entrepreneur)!

The wind is one reason why containers dry out quickly and the plants in them need frequent watering. Other factors are the depth of compost in the pots and the way this can rapidly heat up and lose moisture through the sides of the container; terracotta pots are particularly porous. And while plants in the ground draw their water from natural reserves in the soil, this just isn't possible for plants in pots. When you first fill your containers the plants are small, so they don't need much water. But when summer comes and they start growing like mad, with the scorching sun drying them out at the same time, demand for water greatly increases. If you don't have a regular routine of watering in the morning and the evening your beautiful containerised creations will snuff it!

Even two drinks a day may not be enough; you might need to water a hanging basket exposed to the full sun three or four times daily. Here, you need to take advantage of all the technology you can afford. There are plenty of products on the market to help you to meet these demands – everything from drip-feed irrigation systems and water-retaining gels to hanging baskets with built-in reservoirs. Or you could try something simple and home-made – simply puncture some small holes in the lid of a soft drink bottle, turn the bottle upside down on the pot and it will slowly deliver water when the compost dries out.

ACCESS

How are you going to water your hanging baskets? That's a crucial consideration. You need to be able to get to your containers easily to water them with the least hassle. Once you've heaved a hanging basket into position you won't want to take it down to water it – unless you fancy yourself a bit of a strong-man and enjoy the workout! It is also difficult to hoist a watering can over your head. You could use a plastic jug instead, especially if you've only got one or two baskets. But if you've decked out your terrace with a miniature hanging gardens of Babylon, it can get a bit tedious adding only a jug-full of water at a time. A better idea would be to invest in a special hanging-basket waterer. These pump water up a rigid piece of tube, which hooks over the top of the basket so that water can be delivered straight to where you want it. There are also counterbalanced fittings on the market which allow you to raise and lower the basket easily, yo-yo like, so that you can check it without breaking out into a sweat.

If you've arranged several containers in a group, make sure that the ones at the back can be reached easily with a watering can, without having to move those in front out of the way. I know it sounds obvious, but without a bit of forethought these little hassles can easily become huge irritations, with the result that your gardenless garden ends up more of a chore than a joy.

Above Almost all plants suit a plain terracotta pot – here, the drama of the planting is offset by use of a muted pallette of reds and pinks.

TERRACOTTA

The nice thing about good old terracotta is that it shows off fantastically just about every type of plant. It's what you'd expect, really: after all, the red clay of the terracotta is dug from the same earth that plants grow in. There are tall, big-bellied Ali Baba terracotta pots, broad shallow ones, minimalist modern pots that look fantastic in courtyard gardens and outdoor rooms, ones with restrained patterns and others adorned with Greek figures – you name it, you'll probably find it.

Some of the larger terracotta containers have definite sculptural qualities: they look so good, you almost don't need to put plants in them! Then, as if shape, size and decoration are not enough, clay pots come in an ever-increasing range of colourful glazes. Most attractive of these in my opinion is cobalt blue, a colour which always makes a startlingly eye-catching foil for the green of foliage. Some colours have a perennially satisfying quality, cobalt blue is one of them.

One thing to be mindful of with terracotta is whether or not the pots are frost-proof. Always ask the seller. Good pots tend to be so; mass-produced ones can be dubious. Frost-proof means that the pots will not crack and fall apart during an average winter, when temperatures fall to below freezing. Sometimes a pot looks fine until you pick it up, when it just falls apart in your hands. Containers with colourful glazes are often intended for conservatories and sometimes can't be left outside in cold weather. If you buy a pot and are worried that it might not be frost-proof, wrap it snugly in bubble-wrap come winter, move it out of any exposed position, don't let its base sit in pools of water, and stand it on pot feet.

MATERIAL MATTERS

Years ago your options were limited when it came to buying containers. The choice was between terracotta and plastic, and that was it as far as planters went. The range of shapes was pretty restricted as well – just your typical 'flowerpot' shape. If you had some imagination you'd press into service all sorts of other items, such as old chimney stacks and tin baths, rusty watering cans and kitchen pots, even old boots. This is how country dwellers used to get their containers for free. But in today's era of consumer choice, containers are made from many different materials and come in a huge variety of shapes and sizes – from traditional pots with twee designs to sleek metallic planters. And it often seems as though garden centres, especially DIY outlets, stock more types of containers than plants to put in them.

BRUSH ON THE YEARS

The great thing about terracotta pots is that their looks improve with time. Leave it to nature, and the ageing process happens gradually over months. Salty stains form on the pot sides, green algae and moss gain a foothold, and lichens make brightly coloured splashes. After a season or two, there's nothing to remind you of the pot's brash orange newness. Better still, you don't have to wait for time to work its magic: it's easy to accelerate the ageing process. Just mix some old yoghurt into water, or make up a solution of sheep droppings or horse manure. Next use an old paint brush to apply the mixture to the outside of the container. The coating provides a great growing medium for algae and lichens. Soon the pot will have that been-there-for-ever look.

PLASTIC AND GLASS FIBRE

Plastic pots used to look terrible. I still don't much care for their appearance, but in certain situations they are practical. They don't break if they're dropped, don't crack apart if there's a frost and are not absorbent so don't need as much watering. Also, plastic weighs less than other alternatives, but as a result plastic containers do blow over much more easily if they contain a plant which has a large 'sail-area' (but they won't break if this happens!). You can be creative and paint plastic pots in bright colours, doing a bit of stencilling around the rim. Another clever disguise is to wrap them in flexible bamboo fencing cut to fit, or cover them with anything else which takes your fancy – shells, feathers, stones, mosaics.

Glass fibre containers imitate traditional materials such as stone urns and lead troughs, but they are incredibly light and as such useful for places where weight is an issue. They come in muted naturalistic colours and are strong as well as light, though they will chip if dropped.

WOOD

Timber tubs and half-barrels have always been popular. Large containers can be planted with ambitious arrangements of stately plants. Bamboos, especially *Phyllostachys aureosulcata* var. *aureocaulis* with its yellow culms, look stunning in a wooden barrel. Wood is a good insulator, so the compost is less prone to the fluctuating temperatures of the surroundings, hence the roots of the plants escape extremes of heat and cold. The depth of the containers also means the compost in them retains moisture, so you don't

Above left The timeless quality of terracotta lends itself to classical motifs.
Above Pots made from concrete and stone have a cool, contemporary feel.
Left Metal containers are the ultimate in cutting-edge chic, although planting up an old-style metal bucket will give a more traditional feel.

need to water so frequently. Wooden containers are also versatile: you can seal one with a plastic liner, fill it with water and develop it as a miniature pond for your gardenless garden.

CONCRETE AND STONE

Containers made of these materials should last forever and, although rather hard in appearance when new, they mature well. If you want some permanent fixtures in your gardenless garden, and weight isn't an issue, then a concrete or reconstituted stone trough or urn makes a striking feature. Cultivate trailers such as ivies and lobelias in them – their gentle informality softens the hard edges of the container. And don't forget, any climber will also trail, so you can plant a large-flowered clematis to spill over and round its pot.

Old stone troughs can often be found in architectural salvage yards. They make perhaps the most attractive of all containers – solid and full of character. But beware, you need a deep pocket to buy one and strong springs on your vehicle to transport it home.

GALVANISED METAL

Galvanised metal pots with smooth, straight sides are now very popular. Such pots suit minimalist designs well. You can even have metal troughs deep enough to grow decorative vegetables and herbs. Pots made of metal are nothing if not dramatic. Somehow the ultra-cool demeanour of this material suits common-or-garden veggies very well, but it also looks stunning when planted up with architectural plants, spiky-leaved ones in particular. The chimney bellflower (*Campanula lactiflora*) and the upright silver-green spires of southernwood (*Artemisia abrotanum*) look very effective planted in a tall metal pot, especially when displayed on gravel and decking.

Metal may be an exciting and innovative material, but it heats up madly in hot sun and this may bake the roots. Conversely, the soil in these containers can freeze in winter, so the pots will need wrapping with insulating material. You can't win, can you? That's why metal containers are great for shady gardens. Their reflective surface helps to brighten things up, and because they're not in full sun the plants won't cook.

MATCH-MAKING

Pots are great for growing single specimen plants, marking them out as special. Hostas and ferns, for example, cry out for an individual space, and the former don't get attacked so much by slugs as they do in the open garden. You can cosset treasured exotics by growing them in containers. Oranges, for instance, can be grown outdoors in pots in summer, but they need to be brought into a conservatory or greenhouse in winter, so this makes them ideal tub subjects. On the other hand, many plants look a little lost on their own in a pot. For example, a plant like the grey-green-leaved *Helichrysum petiolare* lacks focus and looks better with others. Recognising which plants look best on their own in a container and which look better with others comes fairly naturally. But matching plants to container shapes is more of an art.

PLANTS FOR DEEP POTS

Tumblers and trailers such as bidens, ivies, nasturtiums, petunias and the less vigorous clematis varieties suit tall pots. So do erect, stately plants such as delphiniums, foxgloves, phormiums and pencil junipers. As well as suiting tall containers, many of the older varieties of lilies, such as the regal lily (*Lilium regale*) which grows up to 1.8m/6ft, need the depth of compost they hold because they are stem-rooters. As the stems of these flowers grow from the bulb, they put out roots into the surrounding medium: without a good depth of

compost, they won't develop a strong root system. Remember, too, that you'll need to support such tall plants with some discreetly placed wire hoops and canes. Some new varieties of lilies, called 'patio lilies', have been developed, which only grow about 30cm/1ft high, so need no support at all. But it's those grand old regal lilies that really do it for me. My balcony's full of them!

Tall 'long tom' pots suit sweet peas grown up a wigwam of canes, or, in a sheltered spot, the classy climber morning glory (*Ipomoea tricolor* 'Heavenly Blue'), the flowers of which are a remarkably intense colour. Trailers such as verbena and upright plants such as standard fuschias, make good companions in a tall container – the trailers forming a skirt around the base of their upright companions.

PLANTS FOR EXPOSED SITES

Bamboos and other tall grasses such as *Miscanthus sinensis* 'Morning Light', *Fargesia nitida* (syn. *Arudinaria nitida*) and *Fargesia murieliae* make good windbreaks for roof and balcony gardens. Their tough resilient leaves are not easily damaged and more fragile plants will grow in the shelter they afford. If privacy is an issue, they also screen your garden from view. Other good choices for an exposed roof garden are cotoneasters, viburnums and hollies, along with the escallonias and *Griselinia littoralis*, both originating from windy environments. Lavenders (*Lavandula*) are also surprisingly tolerant and add a splash of colour.

PLANTS FOR SHALLOW POTS

Wide, shallow containers show off plants with dense mats of foliage, such as houseleeks (*Sempervivum*), with their fleshy grey-green leaves and unusual forms, and helxine (*Soleirolia*), a tiny-leaved, vividly green carpeting plant that forms perfect mounds. Its common name is 'mind-your-own-business', an oblique reference to the fact that if you poke it with your finger it leaves a dent! Contrasting pots of small grasses would add a touch of humour to such a collection of low-growing plants.

Small spring bulbs planted en masse look beautiful in shallow pots. Choose yellow or purple crocuses and don't be afraid to plant the bulbs so that they touch one another. Once the spring bulbs are finished they can be replaced by petunias or tumbling annuals such as bidens or helichrysum, then lilies. Think of each arrival as a flamboyant character suddenly announcing itself on stage. Pale pink autumn crocuses (*Colchicum*), planted in groups of three to an 18cm/7in pot, will provide a dramatic splash of colour in the autumn. You can raise low-profile displays like these to prominence by placing the containers on a staging, such as the rungs of an old stepladder.

PLANTS FOR SQUARE POTS

With a big, chunky square container you can create an entire gardenless herb garden! Most herbs don't require brilliant soil and will withstand exposure to the elements. Plant lavender, bay, rosemary, thyme, sage, French tarragon, winter savory and oregano in one – they're all perennials and some of them have attractive variegated forms. When summer arrives, introduce annuals – coriander, basil, summer savory, parsley and

Left Sempervivums and other succulents need a layer of grit under them to help prevent rotting.

Any plant can be grown in a pot, provided the pot's big enough

chives – to supplement your supply of herbs for the kitchen. Mint is made for growing in pots, simply because you daren't plant it in the open garden, where it spreads like anything and soon takes over. It's also too invasive to go in a pot with the other herbs and needs solitary confinement. A collection of mints, each grown in a 20cm/8in pot, will bring scents you hadn't dreamed of to your nose. There's pineapple mint, which smells exactly like the fruit, peppermint, spearmint and eau de cologne mint (okay, so that's not a culinary one, but it smells great!). Thymes and sages also have similarly aromatic families.

In the case of a roof garden, group containers of herbs together in a sunny position, and protect the more tender ones, such as rosemary and French tarragon, in winter. You can do this most effectively by bringing them inside and placing them on a sunny windowsill until the worst of the winter frosts have passed. If this isn't an option, cover the surface of the compost with a thick layer of mulch to help it retain heat and, if necessary, wrap the pot in horticultural fleece – if you can't get that, chunky bubble-wrap is a good alternative – so that the soil doesn't freeze and kill the roots.

PLANTS FOR BASKETS

Good choices for hanging baskets include trailing geraniums, fuchsias and petunias. Herbs also do well in the confines of a basket; many of them originate from dry places with little soil. Prostrate rosemary, basil and thyme – especially the variety 'Doone Valley' – can be packed cheek-by-jowl into a hanging basket. Prune the excess growth by picking it off and eating it! You can also use plastic hanging pouches for herbs, as long as you plant a few frothy trailers, such as nasturtiums, in amongst them to cover the plastic.

Far left Bamboos thrive in large containers, provided you keep them well-watered. **Left** Bright-faced pansies and trailing ivy make perfect partners for a hanging basket.

Above Deep metal barrels provide the right depth of soil for tree roots, allowing trees to be grown almost anywhere!
Above right Try heathers for good autumn pot colour.

TREES FOR TUBS

Trees take quite well to containers, but you have to pick your specimens carefully. Conifers, especially the slow-growing and dwarf varieties, always look good, as do many Japanese maples (*Acer palmatum* varieties). Box and bay (*Buxus* and *Laurus*) trees can be clipped into formal shapes, making them naturals for a tub, while the golden-leaved false acacia (*Robinia pseudoacacia* 'Frisia') will greet early spring with its bright foliage. Though not strictly trees, bamboos have a similar presence and most will thrive in pots.

Many ornamental fruit trees also do well in tubs, such as the morello cherry (*Prunus cerasus*) and dwarf apple trees. If you live in a warmish climate and have a sunny spot for it, fig trees (especially *Ficus carica* 'Brown Turkey') do well in tubs as they don't need huge containers. In fact, 'Brown Turkey' is one plant you won't have to pot on each year, for it positively thrives on an ultra-restricted root-run. As long as it is watered and fed well when the fruits are growing, it will do famously, and there's nothing quite like plucking your own sun-warmed fig of a summer morning! Even more exotic for a sunny, sheltered position would be an orange or lemon tree, though they must be moved inside over winter.

POTTING UP AND TAKING CARE OF YOUR PLANTS

So you've chosen some containers for your gardenless garden and the plants you want to grow in them. But before you start filling the containers with compost, there are a couple of other jobs to do.

With terracotta pots it's a good idea to 'condition' them before planting up, particularly in summer. Simply soak the pot in a bowl, or if it's large dunk it in the bath (on a folded newspaper so the pot doesn't scratch the enamel) and let it sit there for a while. If you don't condition it, the pot will absorb much of the first watering you give your plants, and you don't want that to happen, so give your terracotta a drink first!

Check that a metal container has drainage holes. If it doesn't, turn it upside down and drill some holes through the base; this ensures that any ragged edges made by the drill bit will be on the inside of the container. And remember: always wear safety goggles when using a power drill.

Start potting up by putting a layer of drainage material in the bottom of the container, taking care not to block the drainage holes. Bits of broken flowerpots and gravel are the traditional materials for the job, but chunks of broken polystyrene board or the polystyrene granules used as packing material are weight-saving alternatives. As long as the material is inert and does its job, plants are not fussy. But it's a different matter when it comes to the growing medium or compost.

MAGIC MIXTURES

Growing mediums for pots need to be tailor-made for the limited environment. You can't dunk a load of garden soil in a pot and expect your plants to thrive (unless your soil is magical stuff). Pot plants need a soil that's moisture retentive, yet drains well, and has a good supply of nutrients. Soil-less and multi-purpose composts do the job well enough. Choose peat-free mixes; apart from the environmental damage peat extraction causes, it can be the very devil to re-wet once it has dried out. For hanging baskets use a soil-less compost because it's lighter. Proprietary mixes soon run out of steam nutritionally, so add some seaweed meal to the mix, following the instructions on the packet.

HOW TO DO IT

When you're transferring plants from plastic pots to containers, make sure no more of the stem gets covered than before. Put a sufficient layer of new compost in the container. Next remove the plants from their plastic pots and position the rootballs on this layer of compost. Firm more new compost around the plants until it reaches the point on the stem covered by the compost in the plastic pot.

When you're planting a single specimen plant, put the plant still in its pot into the container to get an idea of height and placement, position it, then fill in all around with soil, pressing down the compost firmly round the potted plant. Gently ease your plant out, pot and all, and pop the rootball back into the ready-made hole, which will be exactly the right size! This means no disturbance to the roots at all, but firm in well. Aim to leave 2–5cm/1–2in between the rim of the pot and the surface of the compost. Otherwise, when you water half your soil will run off! Water in well after planting to help the plants get established.

Permanent displays of shrubs, perennials and bulbs growing together should be planned to take account of how the plants will develop. Half-fill the container with compost when initially potting up, position the plants on this layer and firm in more compost around them. Every other year, lift the plants without disturbing the rootballs, add some fresh compost to the bottom layer and replace the plants. That way, plants grow into their containers.

There's a bit of a mystique about planting up hanging baskets. The trick is to remember that these are temporary displays and break all the

Above left Press in the compost around the plant so that it feels firm. Remember to leave a small gap between the soil surface and the top of the pot – so that water doesn't drain off the edges.
Above One of the gardenless gardener's most exciting moments: knocking your purchases out of their plastic pots before planting them in their chosen containers.

rules of spacing: cram the plants together. This means that the number of plants needed for the average 35cm/14in hanging basket can prove quite expensive, but there are ways to save money. If you're horticulturally minded you could always try raising your plants from seed – but this can be tricky and laborious, plus you'll need to start in early spring if they're going to be ready in time for summer. An easy way of saving money is to use an inexpensive moisture-retaining layer of plastic to line the basket instead of the moss usually recommended – the plastic can be disguised with dried reeds or grass.

Once the plants are firmed into place, reduce moisture loss by covering the surface of the compost with a layer of mulch. Gravel, pebbles, glass beads, bark and cocoa shells – all sold by garden centres – make good mulches.

SECRETS OF SUCCESS

Container plantings start out as perfect little gardens and it is important to keep them looking that way. In the flower border you haven't the time to tidy up religiously, nor do you need to: a certain informality is fine. But plants growing in containers are on display and in the public eye. Make sure you dead-head annuals regularly, carefully picking off flowers that are finished and nipping off seedheads to extend the flowering season as well as keep the display looking tidy. Picking off yellowed leaves and removing debris from the surface of the compost also keeps things neat, as does sweeping the ground around the containers.

In the case of permanent plantings, add some slow-release fertilizer granules to the compost at the start of the second growing season, forking them gently into the surface. Select fertilizers that are high in phosphates and potash to produce strong roots and tough growth, and avoid high-nitrogen fertilizers, which promote the sort of sappy, lush growth that can encourage disease. Follow the instructions on the packet.

Container-grown plants are prey to the same pests as their garden neighbours. But because they receive more attention you should be able to spot trouble earlier. One particularly troublesome pest is the vine weevil; for some reason it makes a beeline for containers. The grubs attack the roots, causing your cherished specimens to suddenly wilt and keel over. Chemicals will kill them, but a better choice is an environmentally friendly nematode, a natural parasite. You have to order this from a supplier. The nematode eggs, delivered by post, are mixed in a watering can and sprinkled onto the compost, where they hatch. The containers will smell peculiar for a few days, but I recommend you give your specimen plants and long-term container plantings a treatment every summer.

PLANTS FOR CONTAINER DISPLAYS

PERMANENT PLANTINGS

Juniper (*Juniperus communis* 'Compressa'): erect specimen plant.
Lonicera nitida 'Baggesen's Gold': decorative, small-leaved horizontal shrub.
Hebe 'Bowles' Hybrid': evergreen small-leaved shrub, with purple flowers May to September.
Bergenia cordifolia: large paddle-shaped leaves and pink flowers.
Cordyline australis 'Purpurea': a red sword-shaped leaved cabbage palm.
Hedera helix 'Goldheart': trailing ivy with yellow-splashed soft green foliage.
Euonymus fortunei 'Silver Queen': small variegated shrub with silver and green foliage.
Colchicum 'The Giant': autumn crocus with pale lilac flowers.
Crocus tommasinianus: early purple crocus.

SPRING CONTAINERS

Crocus ancyrensis: small early crocus with up to three golden yellow flowers per stem.
Narcissus 'February Gold' or 'Tête-à-Tête'.
Muscari armeniacum (grape hyacinth): spring bulbs with globular, blue flowerheads.
Tulips: thousands of garden hybrids to choose from.
Polyanthus variabilis: primula with deep red and golden yellow flowers.
Viola 'Universal Mixed': a pansy flowering from late Autumn to Spring, which comes in various colours.

SUMMER CONTAINERS

Fuchsias: vast selection to choose from, including the varieties 'Springtime' and the trailers 'Cascade' and 'Pink Galore'.
Impatiens: the busy lizzies bear multicoloured or single-colour flowers.
Lobelia 'Sapphire': classic blue trailing lobelia ideal for summer containers or hanging baskets.
Petunia surfinia: a trailer which comes in an amazing range of colours.
Helichrysum petiolare: grey-leaved trailer, foliage provides a great foil to other plants.
Pelargoniums: perhaps the most widely grown flowers in balcony gardens and hanging baskets.
Bidens: yellow-flowered sprawler which knits things together.

CHOOSING THE RIGHT PLANTS FOR YOU

Before you even start looking for plants, here's a warning – you'll be spoilt for choice! The plant world is vast, mind-bogglingly so. There are so many plants out there it's liable to put you in a spin. And for the new gardener this can be a bit daunting – so much choice means a lot of decision-making. It's a vital process, though, and shouldn't be rushed. I can't stress enough how important it is to devote plenty of time and thought to choosing your plants. The plants you select now will determine how your space looks in the months and years to come. Pick your plants well, and you will be constantly wowed by what you've created. Rush out to the garden centre and make loads of impulse buys and chances are you'll end up with a bunch of costly mistakes.

PRACTICAL CONSIDERATIONS

SOIL AND CLIMATE

When purchasing plants there are several factors to consider. Firstly, the variety of plants you can grow will be governed by the soil and microclimate in your little piece of the urban landscape, be it garden, roof terrace, or window box. Ask yourself, 'Will this plant be able to grow happily where I want to put it?' For example, there's no point growing *Clematis armandii* on a north-facing wall – it won't survive the winter. It's a sun-lover and likes a warm, protected climate all year round. Give it the right position (full sun in a relatively protected spot), and it's a beauty.

DEALING WITH A POOR SITE

Although I am dealing mainly with the 'standard' urban garden, you might have the urban space from hell. You know the type: pylons to the left of you, electricity sub-station to the right, railway line at the bottom, and soil made up of clinker straight out of the devil's furnace itself. If so, you probably need help from the gods... but there are still plants which will alleviate most of your problems.

If you are troubled by wind, then there are some good evergreen trees you can use as windbreaks: the common holly (*Ilex aquifolium*), or some of its more beautiful cultivars like *Ilex* x

BEFORE BUYING A PLANT

Before buying any plant, think **WALNUTS** : **W**ater, **A**ir, **L**ight, **Nu**trients, **T**emperature, **S**oil. Then evaluate which of the plants you would like to buy will actually suit the conditions of your space. Here's an example to show you what I mean. Take an English classic, lavender:

- **Water:** lavender likes free-draining soil, and tolerates drought well.
- **Air:** it has good pollution tolerance, so is great for urbanites to grow.
- **Light:** being Mediterranean in origin, it prefers full sun.
- **Nutrients:** it prefers fertile soil when young, but thereafter will take care of itself.
- **Temperature:** surprisingly, given its origins, it's very hardy, and will tolerate fairly low temperatures as long as it's in full sun.
- **Soil:** should be free draining, which means it likes soil with grit or gravel in it (not thick clay!). It's not fussy as to acid or alkaline soil. It can successfully be grown in containers as long as you provide a soil which drains freely.

Using this simple acronym, WALNUTS, and applying it to every plant on your wish list, means you shouldn't go far wrong.

altaclerensis 'Camelliifolia Variegata' or 'Belgica Aurea'; the bay tree (*Laurus nobilis*); or the Western red cedar (*Thuja plicata*). That cedar will also quickly screen unsightly objects, as will *Chamaecyparis lawsoniana* 'Green Pillar'. If you think your screening trees are lacking colour or scent, grow a climbing rose or clematis through them – they'll provide extra interest.

There are lots of choice evergreen shrubs which will withstand wind, too: barberry (*Berberis darwinii*), Mexican orange blossom (*Choisya ternata*), *Griselinia littoralis*, lavenders, pittosporums, rosemary, *Brachyglottis* 'Sunshine' (syn. *Senecio* 'Sunshine'), tamarisk. Even some roses, such as *Rosa gallica* var. *officinalis* and *Rosa rugosa*, will thrive in windy conditions, as do some bamboos, like *Sinarundinaria nitida,* which seem especially created to complement the built-up urban space.

Polluted environments can also be home to choice greenery: the Hupeh rowan (*Sorbus hupehensis*) is commonly seen lining city streets, as are many of the flowering cherries (*Prunus* varieties). If your soil is lacking vitality, then try herbs, annuals, geraniums and nasturtiums, which all generally do best in poor soils.

ASK THE NEIGHBOURS

Your next-door neighbours – the ones with the urban Garden of Eden, not the ones with the nightmare weed jungle – can also be very helpful. After all, they've already gone through a similar process of selection to the one you're experiencing. They probably have a similar soil and microclimate to yours, and will undoubtedly have already asked themselves the same questions you're currently mulling over. Gardening is one of this country's most popular pastimes. People are always eager to talk about it and offer advice, so take advantage of this. Be friendly and more than likely your neighbours will fall over themselves to help – if you're lucky you might end up with a free plant or two!

MAINTENANCE

Apart from the growing environment, the other big thing I consider before going out on a spending spree is how much maintenance my chosen plant will demand. When a plant is one of my absolute favourites, I personally don't mind devoting time and effort to it (within reason). If, however, you don't want to spend loads of time cosseting plants, select ones which are low maintenance and easy to grow and avoid the fussy ones!

Plants can be fussy for a number of different reasons. They might be a bit tender, which means at the first sign of frost you have to rush out and wrap them up in winter woollies! They might need constant watering during the summer when you'd

rather be sitting with a drink in your hand. Or they might be really greedy feeders and need regular doses of fertilizer to stop their leaves turning yellow.

THINKING ABOUT VIGOUR

Probably the most important factor to consider is vigour, how much growth a plant puts on each year, but don't confuse this with height, as very often knowing the ultimate height something can grow to isn't a great indicator of vigour. For example, the strawberry tree (*Arbutus unedo*), will mature into a whopper of more than 20m/65ft high. Even so, it's still a good choice for the urban garden because it's pretty slow growing and takes years to achieve this height. It might end up big, but it's not terribly vigorous.

By contrast, the Leyland cypress (x *Cupressocyparis leylandii*), a coniferous hedging plant, was spawned by the devil himself. It's the ugliest, most vigorous, and (in my view) the most disgusting plant ever, with no place in any garden, urban or otherwise. Yet you see it everywhere. People are seduced by the fact that it grows so fast, up to 3m/10ft in a year. But forget the pruning for a year or two, and boy, have you got a job for your local tree surgeon – and your neighbours probably won't be too pleased either! Better to choose instead the evergreen Western red cedar (*Thuja plicata*), which looks great, has a lovely aroma and you won't have to sweat buckets trimming several times a year to keep it in check.

Russian vine (*Polygonum baldschuanicum*) is another good example of the plant from hell. Come high summer, it's a beautiful deciduous twining climber, covered in panicles of drooping pink or white flowers. Sounds nice, doesn't it? But it's also known as the 'mile-a-minute' plant. Unchecked, it will easily grow to more than 15m/50ft or more. It's one of the most invasive and vigorous climbers out there and will compete for water, light and nutrients with your carefully nurtured choicest of plants. It's fine for smothering motorway fences, but it's definitely not one for the urban gardener – not for the sane, at least…

If you're seriously impatient, or need immediate impact, go for a mature specimen. You may end up forking out more than you expected, but at least you won't have to grab the machete every time you venture outside.

ANNUALS OR PERENNIALS?

Another major issue that's key to the amount of work you'll need to do is whether or not to plant masses of annuals and biennials. The life-cycle of these plants lasts only one or two years, so if you've got a whole bed devoted to annuals, that's a lot of planting every year, and a lot of money you'll be shelling out too. On the other hand, if you are a restless, creative sort it'll give you an excuse to experiment with ever wilder planting schemes and colour combinations. It's your call. But if you want a nice low maintenance garden, then make shrubs, a tree or two, a generous load of bulbs, and lots of perennials and evergreens the mainstay of your garden. You can always add in a few annuals as the fancy takes you, dotting them around to create new effects or leaving spaces to experiment. As long as you put down a thick mulch to keep the weeds away until the plants have established, the garden will pretty much grow itself.

WHERE TO LOOK

Nurseries and garden centres should be your first port of call when it comes to choosing and buying plants. Your local nursery is often the best place for good advice and quality plants. After all, they've raised and nurtured the plants themselves and as such know how to take care of them, whereas a lot of garden centres buy in their plants and the staff may not be so clued up. Nursery folk tend to be loaded with horticultural experience and enjoy talking about their specialist interests (plants!). They are used to dealing with questions from beginners to experts alike, so you will probably find them more helpful than most other retail gardening outlets.

Some members of staff in the very large garden centres, and especially DIY stores with a separate gardening section, aren't always as knowledgeable as you'd expect. However, if you've found someone who seems to know what they're talking about, don't be afraid to pick their brains.

Below Some garden centres sell a mind-boggling array of pots and other hardware.

WHERE *NOT* TO LOOK

Supermarkets are good for food, not for plants. It makes me cringe walking into a supermarket totally devoid of natural light, to see rows of 'impulse buys' stacked near the entrance. The plants were probably perfect when they were delivered but by the time you come along they'll have been sitting there for a couple of weeks without any care or attention. And as soon as you get them home, they'll probably snuff it. So be warned! Nor am I a great fan of buying plants by mail order or over the Internet, especially when it's from a grower I've had no dealings with. My view is, if you're spending money on a living thing, you need to touch it, feel it, give it the once-over to check it's okay, especially as you're parting with hard-earned cash.

WHAT TO LOOK FOR

By now you've probably made a few decisions about the types of plants you'd like for your urban space. Before you rush out, however, credit card in hand, you need to know what makes a quality plant and how to spot one.

GOOD ROOT SYSTEM

Probably the most important factor affecting plant health is the root system. We grow plants for what happens above ground, but it's the roots that make it all possible. The roots supply most of the water and nutrients a plant needs – and they also anchor it.

If the plant has been grown in a container, squeeze the pot and gently pull it out so you can see the roots. If you can't see any roots, be wary: the plant has not established well, and is therefore a dodgy buy. The same is true if the roots curl dramatically round and round and you can't see much soil, or if there are lots of roots poking out of the top or bottom of the container. In this case the plant's pot-bound from sitting in its container for ages. In all probability a plant like this won't establish well; forget to water it and it may keel over. What you want is loads of little white roots, called feeder roots, just starting to show through; this indicates that the plant's a youngster, and will rocket away once you've planted it!

RESCUING A POT-BOUND PERENNIAL

When it comes to herbaceous perennials (those plants which die back down in winter), it doesn't matter too much if they're a little pot-bound. In my experience, you can hack the roots around a bit – many actually relish this, and it helps to stimulate the formation of those feeder roots. Don't get too carried away, though, and if you do this in a dry spell give the plant plenty of extra watering.

BARE-ROOTED PLANTS

Bare-rooted plants are often much cheaper than their container-grown cousins. If you buy a bare-rooted plant, check it has as much root as possible, and that the roots are well developed and spread out evenly in all directions. Most importantly, only purchase bare-rooted stock when the plant is dormant in winter.

SOIL

If the soil around the plant is bone dry and the leaves are wilting, go elsewhere. Similarly, if it's covered in weed-growth, run for cover. A little algal growth, however, or a small amount of moss, is fine: it probably indicates that the plant has established well in its container.

There is one question now, which I always ask the supplier: has the plant's compost been treated for vine weevil? This is one of the nastiest pests to

Above If you're buying a shrub or tree, look for an even spread of branches.
Left Reinvigorate a pot-bound perennial by gently pulling apart the circling roots.

hit the horticultural world. Recognisable by white larvae in the compost, or by the circular notching on the edge of the leaves left by the adults, this pest really is a nightmare. If you import it into your garden it will seriously affect the health of your plants, especially pot plants: the larvae eat their way through any roots or bulbs they can find. Whether the suppliers have used a chemical control, or have dowsed their soil with a nematode, it is worth buying plants treated for this pest.

GOOD STEM AND LEAF GROWTH

Ideally, you want a compact bushy shape with loads of lush green leaves and shoots spread out evenly. Beware of plants with leaves that look shrivelled, discoloured, smaller than usual, or tinged yellow or brown. The plant probably hasn't been getting enough food and water. Another sign of malnourishment is stunted growth. Have a good look at the plant. Has it put on new growth? Does it look healthy? If at all unsure, leave well alone.

Right Look out for lush green foliage – it's a sure sign the plant has been properly cared for and has established well. **Below** Ensure the plant has a proper label, with the full Latin name and care instructions.

If it's a tree you're buying, make sure the head is spread out well, with branches radiating out evenly. Avoid trees with lots of crossing branches as these branches may rub, creating wounds for disease to enter. Also, check the main stem for scarring. These can be warning signs of a mistreated specimen.

PESTS AND DISEASES

Pests and diseases are the gardener's bugbear, so it's important to check plants thoroughly before you buy. You don't want to end up fighting a battle you can never win, especially one which entails the use of some noxious chemicals. Check for spots, lesions on stems, discoloured or malformed leaves, signs of mould or rust. Avoid those infested with flies, bugs, webbing, scabs or tiny spiders – when you get them home, they'll infect all your other plants.

Some plants are naturally resistant to various pests or diseases, others have resistance specifically bred into them. The plant label should tell you this, or there might be a board detailing specific requirements and any disease resistance. Buy as many resistant plants as possible and there'll be less need for chemicals. For example, if you buy slug-resistant hostas the plants will need less care and attention, will look better, and with the saving in slug pellets you will be able to buy more plants – plus you'll be doing your bit to protect friendly wildlife, which can be poisoned by eating slugs killed with pellets.

HOW MANY PLANTS SHOULD I BUY?

Deciding how many plants to buy depends upon a number of factors: how vigorous they are, how quickly you want your display to mature, what you want your display to eventually look like, how much space you've got, and lastly how much money you've got to spend – though my budget just seems to stretch the longer I stay in the nursery!

If you're planting specimen plants to use as a focal point, always plant them singly or in pairs where appropriate, as when bordering a path. Apart from that I always place plants on their own, if big enough, or in odd numbers like 3s, 5s and 7s. Groupings of odd numbers are easier on the eye, not so linear. I find even numbers look too uniform, too regimented.

The number you plant and the spacing will ultimately affect how much maintenance you might need to do. Over-plant and you'll be fighting a jungle, each plant struggling against the others for water, light and nutrients. Under-plant, and you'll leave unsightly gaps everywhere. The table on the left illustrates the type of spacing I go for. If you follow this rough guide you'll get a great display.

PLANT	DISTANCE APART	NO. PER SQ. M
Shrubs: Dwarf & slow growing	40–60cm/16–24in	2–4
Medium (pittosporum)	90–120cm/36–48in	1
Vigorous (buddleja)	160–180cm/60–72in	2–3 sq. m per plant
Bush roses	40–60cm/16–24in	3–4
Small herbaceous perennials & ground cover plants	20–30cm/8–12in	9
Herbaceous perennials (average)	30–45cm/12–18in	4–9
Herbaceous perennials (vigorous)	40–60cm/16–24in	1–3
Bulbs (large: daffodil)	20–30cm/8–12in	9
Bulbs (small: crocus)	15–20cm/6–8in	25–36

After checking out a plant's requirements and how these fit with conditions in your garden, everything else really comes down to your personal choice. Whatever your slice of the urban environment, when it comes to choosing plants there are three major considerations: colour, scent and form.

COLOUR

Colour is a powerful tool for creating and enhancing mood. More than any other factor we are seduced by colour in the making of a garden. It's the first thing which catches the eye when you visit a famous garden or even just pop to the garden centre.

GLORIOUS GREEN

Flowers can be frivolous, voluptuous, shy, loud, or can just excite your curiosity, yet the most important characteristic of your garden is the colour green. Many gardeners take it for granted. They think of flowers as the main contributors of colour, yet it's greenery which predominates. It's a pity green is so ignored. We really ought to take this colour more seriously!

Green is everywhere in nature. It is the most tranquil colour you can have. It's great for really tiny spaces, turning them into little oases. Apparently it's good for your heart merely to surround yourself with green. Green is present in so many different shades, both bold and subtle, cool and bright: forest green, grey-green, lime green, pea green, soft green, glaucous green... the list goes on and on. If you so desired, you could plant up a garden for its greens alone, and still be awed by the sheer variety of colour.

Green is a mainstay colour. It will see you right through the year, with evergreens providing quiet background interest and really coming into their own in winter and early spring. In summer, too,

green can hold its own, with the pale apple-green leaves of *Hosta* 'Gold Standard', for example. And you can even find green flowers, like the bells of Ireland (*Moluccella laevis*) and the curious green fists of *Helleborus corsicus*.

Green is the backdrop colour *par excellence* – partly the reason it's passed over. The Victorians were well known for their garish plantings of vivid colours, yet they, too, relied on the great power of green to moderate the loudness of their planting

Left All-green planting is never boring, as long as you have a range of shapes and sizes, textures and tones.

schemes. All other colours go with it, so green foliage plants are perfect as neutral 'buffers' between strong colours, letting you experiment with new colour combinations. Flowers with colours that clash are somehow made safe by the green foliage between them, so if you make a 'mistake' it won't look too terrible! Green allows you to play about with colour in the garden; it's the risk-taker's ally.

COLOUR COMBINATIONS

There's no doubt that colour can make the garden come alive, can make it sing. Just as we have colour preferences when it comes to our clothes or interior décor, so we like to carry this on into the garden. As you start to experiment with colour combinations, it's rare you will make a truly terrible mistake, but your evolving taste will soon spot some combinations which don't please as much

---

LEAF COLOUR

If you have a sunny, well-drained garden with stony soil, you'll find plants with silvery-green leaves grow particularly well – such as lavenders, santolina, artemisia, potentilla – because plants with this leaf colour are designed to withstand scorching sun and dry soil. Plants with dark green leaves are often more tolerant of shade – think of laurels, ivies, and the paddle-leaved *Bergenia cordifolia*.

Try out possible plant combinations at the garden centre

as others. That's all part of the creative process of gardening, and you do have the luxury of being able to change things easily by moving plants about. You never know, you might stumble by accident upon some fantastic and truly individual plant associations!

There are few more beautiful sights than a natural meadow in full bloom, where wild flowers pop up in seemingly random fashion. The effect is pure magic! Yet curiously, if we try for a similar effect in our own garden, dotting lots of different plants about here and there, the picture can easily get lost in the making; the result is often haphazard and too busy on the eyes. It is still possible to achieve the polychromatic colour scheme of a meadow, you just need to plant different varieties in odd-numbered groups rather than singly.

You may decide to go sophisticated and have only one colour throughout. Vita Sackville-West's white garden at Sissinghurst has been endlessly copied. This classic blend of silver and white is not an easy choice, though, and you'll find yourself turning down flowers you really like in other colours. White, too, is rarely pure white, but often the palest tint of other colours, and getting these to match might prove harder than you think! It's good to include white in bolder colour schemes, however, as it is another 'pacifier' like green, often a filler in pastel schemes. Gypsophila or *Crambe cordifolia*, for instance, with their clouds of tiny white dots, are so useful because their airy presence fills out spaces, softens and blends.

The planting style of Gertrude Jekyll, a gardener and garden writer who was hugely influential in the late 19th and early 20th centuries, is still popular today. She advocated perennial summer borders planted with great drifts of soothing pastel hues in pink, blue, and white, with hot yellows, oranges and reds used only sparingly – and this is the ideal many gardeners still strive for today. Here the effect is definitely cottage-garden romantic, creating an atmosphere that's relaxed and tranquil, the overall effect nostalgic, soft and harmonious.

Equally, your taste might be for hot and exotic colours – brilliant 'notice-me!' scarlets, yellows and oranges, combined for an effect that's jazzy and vibrating, pulsing with primary colours interspersed with huge green leaves to set it all off. Quiet restraint or bold dynamism: you can create either when you use colour to fashion the mood.

Different colours behave in distinctly different ways. If you use your garden mainly in the evening, plant a lot of white- and pale yellow-flowered plants: the flowers show up like candles as dusk lengthens. In full sun, though, these pale colours can look washed-out. By contrast, red and blue flowers achieve full glory in the midday sun and seem to disappear as it gets darker. So if you want

SEE IT BEFORE YOU BUY IT

When buying plants for colour always try to see the plant in flower, or at least in the correct season, and to get the exact Latin name for the species or cultivar you require. Going on description alone can be misleading, and plant labels are not always wholly informative and can be less than reliable. I once bought some monkshood (*Aconitum*), with no proper description on the labels, thinking its deep blue flowers would do well in that moist shady spot, only to find that the plants I had bought sported dull yellow blooms! I replaced the plants, but it was time and effort wasted.

Above Variety in single-colour planting schemes comes from contrasts in shape, size and habit. Here the spires of foxgloves contrast with the rounded flowerheads of roses.

a garden of red passion, make sure you're around during the day to enjoy it at its vivid best!

Reds, oranges and vibrant yellows are colours to plant at the front of a small border because they draw the eye, and foreshorten distance. In particular, if you plant scarlet at the back, then your border will look thinner than it really is. Better to plant white and blue at the back as these fade into the distance and create the illusion of space.

If you want to be more precise about colour, rather than just relying on your own taste and judgement, consider the colour wheel. Studying the colour wheel is useful if you want to create effects with colour in a more conscious way. You could choose to go for cool colours only, planting gentle mixtures of blues that will all harmonise well. Or you might want a more dramatic effect and go for a complementary scheme which uses two colours directly opposite each other on the wheel, such as blue-violet and orange-yellow. The colour wheel is a useful tool and will help you decide upon colour combinations before you actually plant up a container or border. It'll save so much time moving plants about when they're in flower.

Above Massed planting of yellows and reds produces a 'hot' colour scheme.
Above centre Silvery foliage is the natural companion to white flowers.
Above far right Opposite each other on the colour wheel, yellow and violet make a vibrant contrast.
Right Dazzling colour effects can be created with foliage plants – here, intense blue tones give an ice-cool feel.

THE COLOUR WHEEL
The wheel divides colours into those which harmonise together and those which complement each other. For a blended effect pick colour segments close to each other, like purple and violet or red and orange, which share the same pigment. Complementary colours are opposite on the colour wheel. Use them to create vibrant, jazzy effects to give bold contrasts in planting.

Don't forget the foliage – it's as important as flower colour

Right The startling, luminous red bark of *Cornus alba* 'Sibirica' comes into its own in winter after all the leaves have fallen.

Below When the winter sun falls on the smooth-textured, shiny, purple-red bark of *Prunus serrula*, the effect can be dazzling.

USING PAINTS FOR COLOUR

Take care when using paint colours outdoors. What may work in your house can look odd in your garden! It's much easier to go wrong with a paint colour than a planting scheme - and much more work to put right. If you have a tiny enclosed courtyard, for example, paint the far wall a dark colour. If you paint it white or any other pale shade the wall will appear to come towards you, which is what you don't want, whereas a darker colour will make it seem further away. If you want to paint your planters, consider how the colour you choose will appear. Dark green, found everywhere in the garden, looks wrong painted on the side of a tub. Lime green, however, works fine, though it's bright! Black planters will almost disappear into the rest of the garden. Terracotta is still the classic, but frost-proof glazed planters in Moroccan blue or pale turquoise look great. Cobalt blue is probably the best colour to offset most plants – don't be put off by people telling you it's a cliché. If it works, don't knock it!

YEAR-ROUND INTEREST

It's important to consider what your planting scheme will look like all year round. Grab the crystal ball – or better yet, do a spot of research; the directory in the following chapter will be a good starting point – and work out which plants still look good after spring and summer are past, unless you don't mind your winter garden full of plant skeletons! Go for continuity of display throughout the year, a garden for all seasons. You might choose early-flowering shrubs, winter and spring bulbs, perennials for late summer and early autumn colour, and enough evergreens to see you through the winter.

Don't just think about flowers as being the main providers of vivid colour. Extend the season by making full use of autumn leaf tints. The dying leaves of liquidambar take on the most fantastic array of flame-like colours, as do the many maples and crab apples, and these often hold onto their brilliant leaves for some time. Definitely worth having! And the young spring foliage of some trees can be equally spectacular: copper beeches, maples, and whitebeams look fantastic in the weeks just after leaf-break.

Even in winter you will find colour in the most surprising places. The bark of the dogwood *Cornus alba* 'Sibirica' glows a plum red in the winter sun, especially when you prune it back hard at the beginning of spring. One of my favourites is *Prunus serrula*, a cherry grown for its remarkable bark that is purple-red in colour with a silky smooth texture. When the sun catches it, the effect is to make the tree really stand out among its other deciduous relations. Definitely one plant with a Wow! factor if there ever was.

Along with trees, shrubs form part of the backbone of interest for the year-round garden. Californian lilacs (*Ceanothus*) vary from pale blue to the most intense azure. Planted against brickwork, the colour combination of massed vibrant blue flowers against a rusty red wall is a great combination. Ceanothus do particularly well in a protected urban environment, as do bottlebrushes (*Callistemon*) with their dense terminal spikes of brilliant red or yellow. And don't forget camellias, daphnes, fuchsias, hebes, hydrangeas and roses, which will clothe a garden in colour from palest yellow to deepest blue, from gaudy orange to brilliant scarlet.

Another way to introduce colour, but in smaller doses, is by using bulbs, not only dotted in between permanent plantings of trees and shrubs, but also in small pots to bring early spring cheer. Buy your spring-flowering bulbs in August and pot them up as soon as you can. When in flower these pots can be placed by the front door, or used to brighten up dull areas of the back garden. You don't need many to make a real impact.

In addition to daffodils (*Narcissus*) and tulips, don't forget hyacinths, grape hyacinths (*Muscari*), spring and autumn crocuses, lilies, cyclamen, alliums and loads more. With careful selection you not only get that incredible spring burst, but you can buy bulbs which flower right up to autumn: colchicums, autumn crocuses, lilies, crinums and *Amaryllis belladonna*.

With careful planning you can have something in flower every month of the year. Do make sure, though, that your basic framework plants incorporate at least a few evergreens to hold the stage when flowering is held back by bad weather.

SCENT

Put simply, we urban dwellers have advantages over our country cousins. In our towns and cities we have ready-made protection: the sheer density of buildings both stores heat and slows down the wind – and wind is the enemy to properly enjoying your scented plants. To fully appreciate the perfume of plants, the air must be fairly still so that the scent can hang around. With a few strategically placed scented plants in your garden – by the backdoor, a window or seating area – you'll come home to a proper little 'heaven-scent' oasis.

On the other hand, urbanites might have a great microclimate for growing scented plants, but the air quality in our cities leaves a lot to be desired. Personally I don't want the odour of car fumes lingering in the little sun patch I collapse into after a hard day's battling with the city. This is why it's even more important to maximise what precious

space you have by incorporating masses of scented plants. The smell of diesel buses will be miles away!

But what do you do if your garden space is a roof terrace or a balcony? Does that mean you can't enjoy scented plants? Not at all. There are various ways and means, devious and ingenious, of trapping scent on even a high-rise balcony, so that apartment living can be a fragrant experience too. Use trellises planted up with lots of climbers in your design, and include trees in pots. These will help to create wind-still areas where scent can linger

BECOME A SCENT DETECTIVE

Scent is highly personal – it's a case of one man's scent is another man's pong. So you really have to get out there and use your nose. Become a nosey connoisseur! A lot of people don't know how much fascinating variety there is among fragrant plants. By becoming a scent-detective you will get to know which ones are simply must-haves for your

TYPES OF SCENTED PLANTS

- **Up close and personal** plants have a great scent, but you need to get fairly close to smell it. A lot of these plants are free-scented when planted en masse, or more generous on warm, moist days, but they reward a good sniff too. Roses are typical here, and witch hazels (*Hamamelis*), lilacs (*Syringa*), peonies, pinks (*Dianthus*), magnolias, and smaller bulbs or corms such as *Cyclamen hederifolium* and *C. purpurascens*, or *Galanthus* 'Sam Arnott'.

- **Touchy-feely** plants like to have their leaves crushed to give off their scent. Rub them gently between your fingers to release the scented essential oils. Most of the scented herbs fit this category: lavender, rosemary, thyme, mint, santolina and southernwood (*Artemisia abrotanum*).

- **Free-scented** plants are generous with their scent, letting it go in the air around the plant. Often this is because of the sheer number of blooms on the plant, as with jasmine, or because the plant lends itself to massed plantings, like night-scented stocks (*Matthiola bicornis*). The air around them can be perfumed for some distance.

Left I never tire of the smell of trachelospermum – I've always got to have a sniff!

Top left The flowers of *Cosmos astrosanguineus* give off a chocolate fragrance you can almost taste.

Top centre A carpet of *Cyclamen hederifolium* brings colour and scent in autumn.

Top right As well as its touchy-feely scent, rosemary produces pretty violet flowers.

Bottom left Lilies can fill the whole garden with scent and are perfect for cutting.

Bottom right *Rhodoendron luteum* flowers prodigiously with pungent yellow blooms.

garden, and which ones to ignore. A good tip is to visit your local garden centre once a month throughout the year just to see what's in flower and what smells good. That way, too, you'll be making sure you have something in flower all year round.

In spring, honeyed scents are everywhere, but when summer kicks in the scents are sweeter, stronger. Winter scents are often piercingly sweet and spicy at the same time. It's an interesting phenomenon, but while men go crazy over the honey, musky, polleny-type scents, women go ga-ga over the sweet floral ones.

The senses of smell and taste are linked, too, as you quickly realise when you've got a cold. So it's not surprising we describe fragrances in foodie terms: bubblegum-scented or candyfloss, orange, raspberry, apricot and a host of other fruits. The perennial *Cosmos atrosanguineus* smells exactly like a bar of dark chocolate – never fails to impress!

COMBINING COLOUR AND SCENT

When choosing a plant, most people go for something that catches the eye – brilliant colours usually – and scent doesn't get much of a look in (unless you're my mother). If you choose carefully, however, you can have both colour and scent. Take a trip to the nursery on a lazy summer day, and just smell everything as though it were a game. You'll get some real surprises. You might make the deduction that few red flowers, apart from roses, have much scent – and you'd be right. Whereas a lot of paler flowers, especially white, seem to be pumping it out.

By choosing your plants carefully you can often get scent thrown in for free. If you love roses and that cottage-garden look, then you can choose a rose of your favourite colour, with the longest possible flowering season, and which will tickle your nose into the bargain. A rose without scent is

such a disappointment. Roses can smell very rose-y, or smell like apricots, china tea, even soap, or cold cream! Make sure you go to the nursery in June and July when they're in flower. You'll sniff so many your nose will have a blow-out. But that's the best way to buy scented plants. Otherwise you might end up with something you can't stand, or which to your nose has practically no fragrance at all! The sense of smell is just so personal.

There are so many beautiful flowering shrubs that you can choose not only the colour you want, but include a good dose of perfume into the bargain. Scent and colour combine in the yellow-flowered Ghent group of azaleas, in butterfly bushes (*Buddleja*), rock roses (especially *Cistus ladanifer*), broom (especially *Cytisus* x *praecox* 'Warminster' and *Genista aetnensis*), daphnes, tree heather (*Erica arborea*), old-fashioned roses, magnolias, mahonias, Mexican orange blossom (*Choisya ternata*) and mock orange (*Philadelphus*), the yellow-flowered deciduous *Rhododendron luteum*, *Ribes odoratum*, lilacs (*Syringa*) and most viburnums. The choice is yours!

With perennials, the choice is so wide that here again I think it well worth combining colour and scent as often as possible: catmint (*Nepeta*), *Crambe cordifolia*, daylilies (*Hemerocallis flava*), lupins (especially *Lupinus polyphyllus*), peonies and phlox, for example.

Some bulbs produce the most intensely perfumed flowers in the garden: hyacinths and most oriental lilies like *Lilium regale*, *L. speciosum*, *L.* 'Imperial Silver', *L. longiflorum*. And the scent and colour of tubs filled with lilies in full bloom will knock you dead every time you pass.

SCENTS FOR WINTER AND SPRING

Sarcococca confusa must be one of the most insignificant small evergreen shrubs there is, yet its tiny white flowers release a scent at this time of

year which has everyone hunting it down. Plant this one by your front door and enjoy it as you come and go! Another choice shrub is wintersweet (*Chimonanthus praecox*) with delicate nodding pale yellow bellflowers on bare twigs that flower in January against a warm south wall. A sprig of this will scent a room; it's that powerful. Drab for the rest of the year, you can easily get your money's worth from this winter beauty by growing a summer-flowering clematis up through it.

Late winter to early spring in sheltered gardens signals the flowering of the choice evergreen climber *Clematis armandii* 'Apple Blossom', with its almond scent. This would be great climbing over a sturdy arbour in a spot which catches the sun. *Wisteria sinensis* is another good climber with a powerful scent, flowering on bare stems in early spring – excellent for clothing a wall or climbing up a sturdy tree. As is *Clematis montana* var. *rubens*, an extremely vigorous climber which the scent of nutmegs spilling from its massed pink flowers.

In the spring garden there is the fantastic daphne family, especially *Daphne* x *burkwoodii* 'Somerset'. This is a choice evergreen shrub with long-lasting flowers, though the plant itself is not terribly long-lived and is prone to viral infection. Even so, it's one of my top plants for scent. Spring bulbs usually produce sweetly-scented flowers, particularly *Narcissus* 'Eystettensis', *N.* 'Pencrebar' and most of the Jonquilla daffodils, like *N.* 'Quail' – planted en masse, the scent carries on the air. Don't forget the hyacinth, either, indoors or out.

Biennials like wallflowers (*Erysimum*), Brompton stocks (*Matthiola incana*) and sweet Williams

Above left Wisteria is an incredibly floriferous climber, with a distinctive fragrance. **Above** *Euphorbia mellifera* is worth the effort to grow, for it's honey-scented flowers.

Above The almond-scented flowers of *Clematis armandii* 'Apple Blossom' appear at the end of winter.

(*Dianthus barbatus*), planted out the previous autumn, begin to flower as the days lengthen and produce a heady combination of scent that's most cheering when spring weather is fickle.

Euphorbia mellifera is another plant that's free with its scent in spring. It's a big, round evergreen architectural shrub which suits modern planting schemes well. The sticky, honey-scented flowers are delicious on sunny late-spring mornings. But make sure you keep it protected from anything more than the mildest frost.

SCENTS FOR SUMMER AND AUTUMN

Climbing plants with free scents are great to have along walls and fences. On still days they literally pour their scent into the garden, filling it up like an air freshener does in a stuffy room. Summer free-scents include honeysuckles (*Lonicera*), fine on partly-shaded walls, and the common jasmine (*Jasminum officinale*), flowering from summer to early autumn is good on a sunny one. But beware: not all honeysuckles and not all jasmines smell sweetly perfumed; some are totally odourless.

Powerfully free-scented lilies, such as *Lilium regale* (midsummer), *L. speciosum* var. *rubrum* (late summer and early autumn), 'Casa Blanca' (mid- to late summer), and the Imperial lily strains (late summer) are great to plant in pots where you entertain – they'll make your guests swoon! Some lilies don't release the real wallop of their scent until after late afternoon, so these are a good choice if you are out at work all day and can only enjoy your garden in the evening (or early morning).

Sweet peas grown up wigwams are also generous with their old-fashioned perfume, and, as long as you scrupulously pinch off all the little pea pods which try to form, you'll have flowers all summer long, with plenty left over for cutting.

The unremarkable looking night-scented stock (*Matthiola bicornis*) has the most incredible scent of coconut ice which carries for metres on warm evenings. It's a straggly customer, best grown with other annuals that can hide its lax growth, but it's an absolute must for the scented summer garden.

CHOICE PLANTS FOR SCENT

If you only have a small urban space there's all the more reason not to compromise with second-rate plants, and I know how we urbanites are a trendy lot! So here's my list of the choicest plants – a cut above the common-or-garden varieties you'll see at any old garden centre – which you should keep an eye open for.

SCENTED CLIMBERS
Lonicera caprifolium, *L. japonica* 'Halliana', *L. periclymenum* 'Serotina'; *Clematis armandii*, *C. montana* 'Elizabeth'; *Jasminum officinale*; *Trachelospermum jasminoides*; *Wisteria sinensis*.

SCENTED SHRUBS
Daphne; *Skimmia laureola*; Christmas box (*Sarcococca confusa*); wintersweet (*Chimonanthus praecox*); old-fashioned roses (esp. Gallica roses, Damask roses, Centifolia roses, but essential to smell the rose before buying); *Mahonia japonica*; pineapple broom (*Cytisus battandieri*); *Pittosporum tobira*; *Buddleja alternifolia*; lilacs (*Syringa*); Mexican orange blossom (*Choisya ternata*), and mock orange (*Philadelphus*); *Viburnum* x *bodnantense* 'Dawn', *V.* x *burkwoodii*, *V.* x *carlcephalum*, *V. carlesii*; *Yucca filamentosa*.

SCENTED PERENNIALS
Artemisia; chocolate cosmos (*Cosmos atrosanguineus*); *Crambe cordifolia*; daylilies (*Hemerocallis flava*); plum-tart iris (*Iris graminea*); lupins (*Lupinus polyphyllus*); peonies (*Paeonia lactiflora*).

SCENTED ANNUALS AND BIENNIALS
Brompton stocks (*Matthiola incana*); sweet sultan (*Centaurea moschata*); sweet William (*Dianthus barbatus*); mignonette (*Reseda odorata*); night-scented stock (*Matthiola bicornis*); sweet rocket (*Hesperis matronalis*); wallflower (*Erysimum cheiri*); sweet pea (*Lathyrus odoratus*).

SCENTED BULBS
Amaryllis belladonna; bluebells (*Hyacinthoides non-scripta*); *Crinum* x *powellii*; hyacinths (*Hyacinthus orientalis*); many lilies (esp. *Lilium regale*, the Imperial strains, *L. speciosum*, *L. auratum*, *L. longiflorum*); many daffodils (especially *Narcissus jonquilla*, *N. poeticus* 'Plenus', *N.* 'Eystettensis', *N.* 'Pencrebar', *N.* 'Quail' and *N.* 'Baby Moon').

PLANTS FOR ARCHITECTURAL FORM

What does architectural form mean when it's applied to garden plants? In addition to any other features they may possess, like beautiful flowers or foliage, architectural plants have a sculptural quality. These plants stand out; they make a definite statement. Plants with architectural merit catch the eye. They have presence. You can't miss the dramatic sword-shaped *Phormium tenax* or the distinctive huge green bottlebrushes of *Euphorbia characias* subsp. *wulfenii*. With architectural plants we're talking stage-strutters, actors, primadonnas!

CREATING FORM

Scene-stealers are useful in the garden because they provide the key note which gives definition to your overall planting scheme. Though in themselves they may act like kings of all they survey, when juxtaposed with other plants in a group, they adopt a more egalitarian role by pulling collections of plants together, knitting them into a composition that's enlivening to the eye.

Architectural plants provide form. Place a plant with architectural quality in the middle of a formless mass of plants and immediately the whole group comes alive. A garden needs distinctive elements in it or it will flounder, lacking a point of reference. Even the wildest looking of gardens must have some form, however cunningly concealed, or a formless mess will be the result. Form anchors.

Boldness in design doesn't necessarily need space for its execution and you'll find the small urban garden benefits from having a strong identity. Primadonnas work in a small space because they make that space larger than life, more than it really is. These plants are the great illusionists.

BOLDNESS OF SHAPE

When I think of architectural plants I get a fizzy feeling in the gut; they've got exciting and challenging shapes that wake you up, make you look more closely. Erect sword-shaped plants like *Yucca filamentosa* are so dramatic you wonder if it's safe to approach... These plants are mean and uncompromising and not for the faint-hearted. Keeping the same upright dagger-like form, but infinitely safer, would be *Crocosmia* 'Lucifer' – its leaves won't stab you in the back when you're not looking!

Huge leaves make a statement. A bonus for urbanites with shady gardens is that those exotic and dramatic large-leaved plants are made for you. Big leaves often wilt in the hot sun, but do better in shade. Big leaves like moisture, and they look great around a pond where they will create an atmosphere of a secret den, a tropical hideaway. A friend of mine planted the vast *Gunnera manicata*

Above There's perhaps no more incredible sight than giant fern fronds sprouting out of a tree trunk. But it takes decades for a tree fern (*Dicksonia antarctica*) to reach this height, so expect to pay a princely sum.

by the side of his raised pool. The leaves grew so huge he was able to put a table and chair underneath them, getting both shade on hot days and total privacy from the upstairs windows of his neighbours! Take care though as these giant jungle plants, particularly gunneras and *Rheum palmatum*, can begin to take over and look threatening – but maybe that was your intention in the first place!

Distinctly shaped trees provide strong architecture, too. The small columnar *Prunus* 'Amanogawa' is very suitable for small gardens. Another tree well suited to the city is the hornbeam *Carpinus betulus* 'Fastigiata' whose shape looks like the perfect Aladdin's-lamp flame. Topiary or loosely clipped bay can satisfy the requirement for an architectural anchor in the garden. Box is so versatile, you can clip it into any shape you fancy, but balls seem to work best (unless your taste inclines to steam engines or swans!).

Bold shapes provide

focal points within

softer foliage

LEAF SHAPES

SPIKY: *Phormium tenax*, *Yucca filamentosa*, *Crocosmia masonorum*; irises.
SOFT-SPIKY: bamboos, reeds and grasses; daylilies (*Hemerocallis*).
ROUNDED: hostas; *Bergenia cordifolia*; *Peltiphyllum peltatum*; rodgersia; *Gunnera manicata*.
PALMATE (e.g. horse chestnut): *Fatsia japonica*; Japanese maples (*Acer palmatum* varieties); the scented Mexican orange blossom (*Choisya ternata*); Virginia creeper (*Parthenocissus quinquefolia*); decorative grape vine (*Vitis vinifera* and *V. coignetiae*).
BROAD-LEAVED: rhododendrons; viburnums (especially *Viburnum davidii*); spotted laurels (*Aucuba japonica*); *Hosta sieboldiana* var. *elegans*.
FEATHERY: Southernwood (*Artemisia abrotanum*) and other artemisias; fennel (*Foeniculum*) and dill (*Anethum graveolens*).

PLANT SHAPES

UPRIGHT: *Juniperus virginiana* 'Skyrocket'; *Prunus* 'Amanogawa', an upright flowering cherry; bamboos and grasses; rosemary; mullein (*Verbascum*); foxtail lilies (*Eremurus*).
HORIZONTAL: *Viburnum plicatum* 'Mariesii'; *Cotoneaster horizontalis*; prostrate junipers.
ROUND: hebes; choisya; box and lavender; *Euphorbia mellifera*; *Alchemilla mollis*.
FAN: yucca; phormiums; ferns such as *Dryopteris filix-mas*; *Euphorbia characias* subsp. *wulfenii*.
WEEPING: weeping birch (*Betula pendula*); *Buddleja alternifolia*; caragana.

LEAF TEXTURE

PRICKLY: hollies such as *Ilex aquifolium*, especially the hedgehog holly (*I. a.* 'Ferox'); berberis; sea holly (*Eryngium*); bear's breeches (*Acanthus*); mahonia.
WOOLLY: lamb's ears (*Stachys byzantina*) – children love to stroke this one!; *Hydrangea aspera*; lavender; Jerusalem sage (*Phlomis fruticosa*); *Verbascum bombyciferum*.
WAXY: *Griselinia littoralis*; rhododendrons; *Fatsia japonica*; *Asplenium scolopendrium*.
RIBBED: hostas; *Viburnum davidii*; *Bergenia cordifolia*; *Salix reticulata*.

Far left *Vitis vinifera* – grape vines – are vigorous but valuable urban assets.
Left *Muehlenbeckia complexa* is a tiny-leaved, frothy, mound-forming shrub or climber.
Below far left *Actinidia kolomikta* is a striking climber with leaves splashed with pink and cream.
Below left *Parthenocissus henryana* produces its best leaf colour on a north- or east-facing wall.

PUTTING IT ALL TOGETHER

Imagine a garden full of nothing but sword-shaped leaves. It would be too full on. You'd need some relief, some contrast. A large-leaved hosta planted in front might be the answer; with its wide, curved leaves and low habit, it would act as the perfect foil to sword-leaved plants. And the look of both plants would be enhanced by the contrast they offer to each other – a case of 'I'll scratch your back, you scratch mine'. Add to this smaller-leaved plants with different leaf shapes and textures, and you have a composition. This is the key to using dramatic plants. Contrast them with one another, mix different geometric shapes and textures, entice the eye to travel from one to the other so it doesn't get bored: spiky with soft, vertical with horizontal, smooth with rough.

Since classical times the group of three has been used to create satisfying composition in the garden. One such grouping might be a columnar tree, a round bush and a spreading plant at the base: you could try an upright *Juniperus communis* 'Hibernica', a rounded light green *Choisya ternata* 'Sundance', along with a feathery catmint (*Nepeta* x *faassenii*) spreading at their feet. These three different shapes put together are pleasing to the eye. If you use just two of them there will appear to be 'something missing'.

Architectural form can also be created by planting a lot of the same plant. This is mainly done with those that in themselves are not particularly architectural, like box plants for formal hedging, or

Far right I don't mind tramping right across the city to get my hands on a choice bamboo for the garden.
Right There's nothing quite like *Euphorbia characias* – it has an eery beauty like a plant from another planet!
Below Beauty and the beast – monster gunneras with delicate arum lilies.
Below right On their own irises are shy little things, but plant them en masse and they hog the limelight.

massed daffodils. Using plants in a formal way like this makes for a very definite focal point. Planting in blocks or geometric shapes introduces strong design elements.

However, you don't have to restrict yourself to only one notably architectural plant in the garden. You can make a garden entirely out of strong forms – it's a bit like creating an orchestra using mainly the louder instruments. The secret is to mix them together so that as a group they appear harmonious, but without losing any one plant's individuality. Above all, don't feel overawed by these characters. Be bold. Take risks. It's your garden. Be as outrageous as you please!

TREES FOR THE CITY GARDEN

Trees are vital to the city garden. They act as a focal point, provide privacy, conceal eyesores, attract wildlife and give substance to the planting. In fact, even the most recently planted garden will acquire an air of permanence with a small tree.

So, no matter how tight your budget, consider a tree as an investment. Not only will it be great for the environment (trees help counteract pollution), it will provide another dimension to your garden, creating a sense of proportion and scale.

Not all trees have to be giants, either. There are some fantastic compact trees available that will provide you with screening for eyesores – like the builder's yard next door – and offer fantastic little hideaways and camouflage. Try evergreens like *Magnolia grandiflora* for year-round privacy, or trees with pendulous canopies such as the purple birch (*Betula pendula* 'Purpurea') or the child-friendly *Laburnum* x *watereri* 'Vossii' for sitting under.

For wildlife habitat, try the hawthorn *Crataegus laevigata* 'Paul's Scarlet', or the ornamental crab apple, *Malus* 'John Downie', with its red fruits. The common hazelnut (*Corylus avellana*) is also good. Or go for a tree with a legend: the white-flowered Glastonbury thorn (*Crataegus monogyna* 'Biflora'), reputedly struck from the staff of Joseph of Arimathea; or the Judas tree (*Cercis siliquastrum*) on which Judas hanged himself!

Choose trees with year-round appeal, if you can. A tree in a confined garden must work hard for its space. Try the Tibetan cherry (*Prunus serrula*) and the winter-flowering cherry (*Prunus* x *subhirtella* 'Autumnalis Rosea'). Both flower early, have attractive leaves, great autumn colour and fantastic bark in winter. For really tiny spaces try Hillier's cherry (*Prunus* x *hillieri* 'Spire'), or the upright *Prunus* 'Amanogawa', a cherry tree smothered in pink flowers in the spring.

Most trees can be grown in pots. Restricting the roots will help to control size but you must feed and water them well. Japanese maples (*Acer palmatum* varieties), magnolias, small birches, and apples are ideal for large containers. Do try my favourite, the Chilean fire bush (*Embothrium coccineum*). In flower it really does look like it's on fire.

THE URBAN TREE – *CHECKLIST*

Consider the following:

Size:	have you the space to let it mature?
Vigour:	how fast will it grow?
People-friendly:	is it poisonous (seed, leaves or fruit), will it produce debris (lots of fallen fruit, autumn leaf fall, sticky mildew – like lime trees), or is it very thorny?
Shade:	How much shade will it cast? Small and/or narrow leaves let in more sunlight (eucalyptus, silver birch); large leaves and a dense crown create deep shade.
Year-round interest:	will it look good throughout the year?
Root run:	are the roots invasive, undermining buildings or ruining your lawn?
Maintenance:	how much pruning does it need?
Disease resistance:	is it susceptible to pests and diseases?

1: *Amelanchier lamarkii*
2: *Malus* 'Katherine'
3: *Betula albosinensis*
4: *Prunus* 'Pink Perfection'
5: *Prunus* 'Amanogawa'
6: *Cornus florida* 'Eddie's White Wonder'
7: *Trachycarpus fortunei*

TREES WITH OUTSTANDING AUTUMN COLOUR

- *Betula pendula* 'Youngii' (Young's weeping birch)
- *Cercidiphyllum japonicum* (candyfloss tree)
- *Amelanchier lamarkii* (snowy mespilus)
- *Acer palmatum* 'Sango-Kaku' (syn. *A. p.* 'Senkaki' – a Japanese maple)
- *Malus* (apple – particularly ornamental crab apples)

TREES WITH AROMATIC FOLIAGE, FLOWERS OR SHOOTS

- *Cercidiphyllum japonicum* (candyfloss tree)
- *Eucalyptus* (prune hard to control size and/or keep juvenile leaf shape)
- *Laurus nobilis* (bay tree)
- *Crataegus* (hawthorns)
- *Malus* (apple – particularly ornamental crab apples)

TREES WITH ORNAMENTAL BARK IN WINTER

- *Betula papyrifera* (paper birch)
- *Prunus serrula* (Tibetan cherry)
- *Acer griseum* (Chinese paper-bark maple)
- *Betula albosinensis* var. *septentrionalis* (pink birch)
- *Acer capillipes* (snake-bark maple)

TREES TOLERANT OF EXTREME AIR POLLUTION

- *Acer pseudoplatanus* 'Brilliantissimum' (pink shrimp-maple)
- *Prunus* 'Pink Perfection' (Japanese cherry)
- *Pyrus calleryana* 'Chanticleer' (ornamental pear)
- *Magnolia* x *soulangeana*
- *Amelanchier laevis* (serviceberry)

TREES SUITABLE FOR NARROW URBAN GARDENS

- *Malus tschonoskii* (ornamental crab apple)
- *Betula pendula* 'Obelisk' (fastigiate birch)
- *Juniperus scopulorum* 'Skyrocket' (fastigiate Rocky Mountain juniper)
- *Prunus* 'Amanogawa' (columnar Japanese cherry)
- *Acer saccharum* 'Temple's Upright' (sugar maple)

TREES WITH GORGEOUS FLOWERS

- *Crataegus laevigata* 'Paul's Scarlet' (hawthorn) – spring
- *Magnolia* x *soulangeana* – spring/summer
- *Laburnum* x *watereri* 'Vossii' – summer
- *Cornus florida* 'Eddie's White Wonder' (flowering dogwood) – spring/summer
- *Prunus* x *subhirtella* 'Autumnalis' (winter-flowering cherry) – autumn/winter

EVERGREEN TREES

- *Magnolia grandiflora*
- *Arbutus unedo* (strawberry tree)
- *Trachycarpus fortunei* (Chusan palm)
- *Cupressus sempervirens* (Italian cypress)
- *Pinus sylvestris* (Scots pine)

PLANTS FOR FOOD

Everyone likes to eat fresh vegetables and fruits. Even with the smallest garden you can grow something to tickle your taste buds.

CHOOSING WHAT TO GROW

There are two important things to remember: only grow things you like, and only grow what is suitable for your site. If you have a tiny garden many edibles are going to be out of the question. For example, something like purple-sprouting broccoli needs a lot of space to mature. Similarly, if your garden is shaded by trees, vegetables won't grow well. In fact, to grow vegetables and fruits to their best, you have to give them the sunniest part of your garden, something you might be loathe to do. Think carefully: do you want to turn part of your garden into serious growing space for fruit and veg, or are you content with a few pots full of the more decorative varieties?

Where space is at a premium, it makes sense to grow only those fruit and vegetables which are best eaten when just picked, or which taste so much better when you grow them yourself, or which are uncommon enough to be difficult and expensive to buy. Saving money by growing your own vegetables isn't really a consideration for the urban gardener, unless you have a huge amount of growing space. So don't waste your valuable mini-acre growing cooking onions when you can easily buy these cheaply in your local supermarket!

Carrots and potatoes also fall into this category, as do most other root crops. Remember that roots store well over winter without losing their vitality. Tender baby spinach or saladings, though, will have lost just about everything by the time you get them home from the shops – and these are easy to grow in the smallest of spaces.

Plan on giving valuable garden space to vegetables and fruit which have that Wow! factor because they taste so much better fresh from the garden. Petits pois, in fact peas in general, fall into this category: you can never get a sweet-tasting pea from the shop, I promise you! Runner beans will grow happily in a 35cm/14in plastic pot, with a few tall canes poked down to the base then tied at their tops to make a wigwam. The plants will quickly scramble up to a height of 2–3m/6½–10ft, providing you with ornamental flowers of scarlet and white (runner beans were originally grown in this country for their appearance, not as a food crop). And the beans grow so fast all you have to do is pick and eat them!

Tomatoes are definitely worth growing too. You can pick varieties which taste truly sensational, and come in all colours. They look pretty, can be easily grown in large pots, and produce masses of fruit. There are even varieties specially bred for growing in hanging baskets. Despite what you read about needing in-depth knowledge of rocket-science in order to grow tomatoes, it just ain't true. Tomatoes are tougher than they look! Although they were

Top row, right Great for flavouring roast potatoes, rosemary also produces pretty little flowers.

Top row, middle Both the leaves and flowers of nasturtiums are edible.

Top row, left Lettuce is simple to grow, and with 'cut-and-come-again' varieties you'll have a seemingly endless supply.

Second row, right Cauliflowers take up a lot of space, but they justify a place in the garden for their sheer ornamental value.

Second row, left Courgettes are surprisingly easy to grow and have fantastic, rhubarb-like leaves.

Third row, right Ordinary broccoli doesn't take up so much space as the purple-sprouting varieties.

Third row, left With the crinkly leaves of this cabbage, you can eat your greens and have ornamental foliage planting to boot!

Bottom row, right Make your climbers earn their keep by planting runner beans.

Bottom row, middle Peppers are tricky to grow in our climate, but you should manage it in an urban suntrap.

Bottom row, left Curly parsley has highly decorative foliage and is often grown in flower borders.

Far left Peas and beans are traditionally grown up cane wigwams.

Left Not many people know that courgette flowers are also very tasty – great for colourful salads.

reasonably well fed, my mum's toms were grown in pots far too small for them so they often started to wilt before she got around to watering them. Yet they produced some of the best tomatoes I've ever eaten. Of course, she could have cosseted them, and so gained a bigger crop. But treating them mean gave those tomatoes that real concentrated flavour. Even now I can remember that taste of a home-grown tom, still sun-warm, popped straight in the mouth.

Other 'easies' are courgettes. They do well in a tub, and with their huge architectural leaves look quite exotic. Yellow courgettes, instead of the common green ones, complete the picture! And, of course, the flowers are considered a delicacy, as well as the fruit.

If your garden isn't overrun with slugs, then it's worth growing lettuce. Even easier than trying to get a whole lettuce to maturity is to grow thickly sown rows of cress, rocket, summer purslane and other saladings. These can be bought in mixtures which you sow thinly on fine soil, and they'll grow happily in a window box, so no excuses, flat-dwellers. You pick leaves as you require, while they're young and tender. Growing the Chinese saladings over winter (they have names like 'Oriental Saladini') is one way to have fresh mini-greens for salads and stir fries out of season. These work exceptionally well grown in deep trays of good friable soil. They seem immune to pests, and grow thick, green and lush.

FOOD AMONG THE FLOWERS
Unlike gardens in the country, where a dedicated vegetable plot can be separate from the main garden, and where you still have space to grow your flowers and shrubs near the house, the smaller city garden usually has to perform many functions. Even in the smallest urban space you can still grow vegetables in among the flowers; choose the more decorative varieties, and they can be attractive and garden-worthy in their own right. Some, such as carrots with their feathery tops, or beetroot, especially a variety called 'Bull's Blood', will grow quite happily among the marigolds, and you would hardly know they were there.

Sneaking garlic around your roses is a great way to keep them free of aphids, which can't stand the smell! And you have the bonus of pulling your own garlic in late summer, too – there's nothing like a fat, juicy clove of garlic, fresh out of the ground, to give your cooking a real kick. Garlic is so easy to plant, it qualifies for a place in the laziest gardener's regimen. In autumn, just poke the individual cloves down about 7cm/3in, and smooth the soil over. That's it! Though you need to use garden-centre cloves, as the supermarket varieties are usually less hardy continental varieties.

Above If you have kids who turn their noses up at veg, grow this pink cauliflower and they'll eat it for the novelty!

If you like the pepperiness of rocket, you'll love the distinctive flavour of nasturtium leaves! Picked small and torn into a salad, these are deliciously piquant. You can eat the flowers too; and the seeds, pickled, taste just like capers. In fact, a number of flowers are edible: rose petals, daylily buds (but who would want to sacrifice the flowers?), and the orange petals of the pot marigold. Some flowers are poisonous though, so don't eat everything in your garden!

One flower which is definitely tasty is the giant flower of the globe artichoke. This monster plant looks fantastic in the garden, especially at the back of a sunny border. You can have the best of both worlds here: pick and cook some flowerheads before they open, and let some grow into full bloom.

GROWING FRUIT
If you want to grow fruit try apples and plums grown on dwarfing rootstocks (these can also be tub-grown), or strawberries in a barrel or large pots. Using alpine strawberries as a decorative edging for your borders is another way to introduce tasty fruit, and these are much better behaved than ordinary strawberries (and the birds don't go for them either!). If you have a bigger garden area devoted to fruit, you might try raspberries. These don't travel well and are sometimes hard to find in shops, so they really are a delicacy. A boysenberry is a blackberry-like fruit (but much larger and juicier) that will grow in most sunny spots and will give you just masses of fruit: train it up a 3m/10ft-tall rustic pole in full sun.

GROWING HERBS
Every garden has space for culinary herbs. You can grow these on the smallest windowsill, in a window box, or on a balcony. These are so easy to

Above Raspberries need a lot of space to grow and regular attention, but the end result is well worth it – if the birds don't get there first!

grow as long as you give them the right conditions. Most like full sun and good drainage. If you have a permanently dry sunny spot, plant it up with rosemary, sage, French tarragon and oregano. Herbs are expensive to buy and, because you need so little of them to transform your cooking, they're really worth the effort. They don't take up much space, either. Mint is such a doddle, it'll grow almost anywhere, so you have to contain it in an old butler sink or similar, to stop it taking over the whole garden!

Basil can be a tricky herb to grow. I find it best to start it off on a warm kitchen windowsill. It hates being watered from the top (the seedlings will keel over and die), so water carefully by filling a pot-saucer underneath, and you should have few problems. When you come to separate the seedlings (pricking out, it's called), my advice is that you don't try it with basil. Instead, gently ease out the whole root ball from the pot and plant the whole thing in a larger pot or in a warm border. If things start to look crowded you can always gently thin them out later.

LITTLE FARMERS

Children in particular love to grow edibles, especially if they are fast growing or big! The pumpkin might take up a lot of room, but smaller squashes easily climb over arches and produce lots of bright colourful fruit to be admired and to eat. Make sure you give your children's patch the very best soil – children easily get discouraged by failure, and won't want to try again. If you can't spare the space, give your kids a couple of large pots to look after. Runner beans grown up a wigwam of canes look pretty dramatic, and evoke 'Jack and the Beanstalk' magic. They are so prolific your children will feel very proud of their contribution to a meal! If you have spare room, your children will love to grow early potatoes in large tubs. Give them good soil as always, and watch their faces when they tip out the barrel and hand you their crop!

HOW TO GROW YOUR EDIBLES

Most plants, other than roots, do better if they're started off indoors in late spring on your sunny windowsills (unless you have a greenhouse). Wait till your baby plants are quite strong before planting them out. That way they will grow away strongly.

You should give your vegetables the best possible soil: better than that in your flower borders. Dig in as much compost as you can spare: a barrow load per square metre for starters. They love compost. If you don't get the soil really humus-rich right from the start, don't even think of growing things to eat because the results will be so measly you'll never want to grow edibles again!

Vegetables also need feeding and watering throughout their lives or you'll get wizened, tough specimens which you won't want to eat. Water saladings especially well because they can get horribly stringy otherwise. Grow organically if you can. Use natural seaweed sprays to boost your plants' vitality and help keep them disease-free. If you see pests munching your veg, don't despair or reach for the pesticide. Caterpillars can be picked off by hand (and fed to the goldfish in your pond!). Greenfly millions can be easily knocked off by water, with or without a little soft soap in it: they'll fall to the ground and get eaten by predators. Remember that the healthier your plants – which actually means the healthier your soil – the less you'll be bothered by pests and disease. So it pays to concentrate on giving plants a healthy soil for starters. I just can't emphasise that enough.

KEEPING YOUR PLANTS HEALTHY

When buying your plants, make sure you don't forget to buy the fertilizer or compost at the same time, if you haven't been 'making' some already (see pages 34–5). Most plants will initially need a regular feed (maybe once or twice a year) to keep them looking the business, so make sure you're well stocked. Ignoring the needs plants have for nutrients will only lead to premature death or sickly looking specimens

FERTILIZERS AND FEEDING

Like all living things, plants need food or nutrients to keep themselves healthy and strong. Generally nutrients can be divided into two groups: the major and minor nutrients. The major nutrients consist of nitrogen (N) for shoot growth, phosphorus (P) for root growth, and potassium (K) for healthy leaves and fruits. The micro-nutrients, often known as trace elements, consist of boron, magnesium, iron, manganese, copper, molybdenum and zinc, all of which are just as important as the major nutrients.

Manures such as garden compost, seaweed and composted chicken manure are excellent sources of both major and minor nutrients; they will also help to condition the soil if it's poorly structured or too free-draining – some are even available in dried granular form for easy application. At the garden centre there is an enormous range of fertilizers in granular or powdered forms. Growmore, blood, fish and bone, and tomato fertilizer are among the best all-rounders available. A good source of both major and minor nutrients,

Above Gorgeous, sweet-smelling compost. There's nothing quite like it and plants just can't get enough!

fertilizer. Don't be tempted to feed in autumn or winter, it'll only promote young tender growth which will be probably be killed by a hard frost. For new plantings incorporate some fertilizer in your planting mix, and for mature plants rake in a little top dressing around each one to help sustain them year after year.

HOW MUCH TO APPLY

How much you apply should be governed by one thing – what it says on the packet. You'll find the application rate, the nutrients it contains, and any other specialist information on the side. Don't be tempted to ignore the application rate – give the plant too much and you might well scorch the roots, poison the plant or cause rapid and unsustainable weak growth. And applying too little is a waste of time – the plant doesn't get the amount it needs (but at least you won't kill it!). The packet is your god. If it says apply 40 grams per square metre once a year, then that's what you do. Get some scales, a measuring stick, and obey!

LOVELY COMPOST

If you haven't the luxury of your own garden compost you can buy numerous types at your local garden centre. Soil-based composts such as the John Innes range are usually high quality sterilised garden loams. They have excellent nutrient and moisture-retention characteristics, while also encouraging good air movement and drainage. Though more expensive than their peat-based counterparts, soil-based composts are ideal for long-term containers (plants you're not going to re-pot every year).

Soil-less composts are typically only used for lightweight short-term mixes, for half-hardy annuals which you replace every year. Alternatively, a couple of good handfuls mixed into your garden soil acts as a soil conditioner, helping your plants acclimatise to their new home. Peat-based composts are well aerated and moisture retentive, but they don't hold onto nutrients easily. They are also notoriously difficult to rewet once dry, so keep container plants well watered. If they do dry out, copious amounts of luke-warm water will help, as will soaking the pot up to soil level in the bath. Peat composts are also environmentally damaging, as the peat is extracted from peat bogs, causing vital natural habitats to be destroyed.

More eco-friendly multi-purpose composts incorporate coir as their bulk constituent. Coir is the fibre from coconut husks, and is often used as a peat substitute although it requires more feeding. Ericaceous (lime-free) composts are also available, allowing you to grow acid-loving plants in containers if your soil is very alkaline or chalky. Select the right compost and your plants will romp away!

Above If you've got a spare shady corner in the garden, there's really no excuse not to make your own compost.

they can be used for almost all plants. Nowadays controlled-release fertilizers such as Osmocote or Ficote are very popular. They release their nutrients over a set period of time, say eight months, meaning you don't have to worry about feeding for that period. While more expensive, controlled-release fertilizers are ideal for hanging baskets or container plants and some are available as plugs which you simply insert into the container – dead simple! There are also specialist fertilizers, tailored to specific plants: orchids, cacti, citrus fruit, acid-loving plants, container and hanging basket plants, for example. They will help you to select quickly and with confidence.

WHEN TO APPLY

It's a good idea to feed at least once a year, ideally in spring when plants are actively growing. However, plants in containers may require extra feeding if you're not using a controlled-release

THE GOOD,
THE BAD
& THE UGLY

Plants are the most exciting aspect of gardening. They give pleasure quite unsurpassed by any extravagant feature or piece of hard landscaping. Plants are living elements we can cultivate and encourage. We can put our time, effort and passion into living, breathing beings. Just how cool is that! The plants we like, and those we don't, come down to one thing – personal taste. It might be shape, flower, form, or even memories, which evoke strong feelings of pleasure or even dislike. Take one of my all-time favourites *Euonymus alatus*, the winged spindle. Why do I like this plant so? Apart from its autumn colour and corky ridged branches, it's a fairly unassuming deciduous shrub, one unlikely to make the top ten list of most gardeners. But to me it has a history which makes it special. It was the first plant I ever propagated successfully. Because of that I always look at it fondly, and try to include it in gardens wherever I can.

The plants in this chapter are my own personal choices, and I've divided them into three categories which I call the good, the bad and the ugly. What I call bad you might love, and what I call ugly might be the ultimate inspirational plant for you! So don't worry. These plants are just a collection I have strong feelings about. Saying what I feel about these plants might help you to think about what you should choose for your urban garden.

THE GOOD...

Plants featured under this heading are some of my favourites, and warrant inclusion in any garden, urban or otherwise – as long as you've got the right microclimate, soil and the correct pH. All are multifunctional plants, meaning they're renowned for more than one attribute – this might be a great fragrance coupled with attractive foliage, or autumn colour and bark to die for. Remember: urban gardens are often small, so plants must be seen to work hard for their space.

THE BAD...

Confusingly, I actually adore some of the plants listed here, and if I had a large garden some of these specimens would be automatic purchases. But these plants are not totally suited to small urban gardens, so I've tried to list more appropriate alternatives; you don't want to end up with a triffid

when you thought you'd bought a non-invasive, well-behaved little thing!

Sometimes, as an urban gardener, you'll want to, or have to, put plants into places where they are not ideally suited. It can be inevitable – especially if your garden is tiny. The plants featured in this category may be worthy of inclusion in your garden, but they need careful consideration – many are fussy, or grow into monsters.

...AND THE UGLY!

Whoever said gardeners didn't have strong opinions! Ugly plants are my pet hates, and the ones listed here should never, in my opinion, appear in gardens, unless they are used as compost! Some of the dullest, most uninspiring, featureless plants are in this group – and I'm sure this is the section you'll turn to first. I only mention them out of sympathy, so you don't waste money and get lumbered with a monstrosity. Approach these plants with caution! And don't say I never told you so...

There are many plants that I love – and I couldn't possibly fit them all in these few pages! So, I've limited this section to some of my absolute favourites, which are also perfect for growing in an urban garden.

Acer griseum

Maples make good trees for small gardens, being neat and ornamental and not too vigorous. The Chinese paper-bark maple is slow growing, and tolerant of either chalky or acid soil. It likes sun but will also thrive in shade, and can be grown in a large tub. In summer the tree will give a spreading canopy of green but in autumn the leaves turn scarlet and orange before falling. The bark is this maple's most striking feature. The rich cinnamon-brown bark peels away in rolls to expose the new copper-coloured bark underneath. This is unusual and quite spectacular in winter when the tree is leafless. Best grown in a sheltered position and protected from heavy frosts. Looks lovely underplanted with red-leaved shrubs and herbaceous perennials such as *Heuchera micrantha* var. *diversifolia* 'Palace Purple' or rodgersia, which pick up the colour of the bark.

Acer palmatum

This is one of the most commonly grown of the ornamental maples and it has fine, palmate leaves. Like *A. griseum* the Japanese maple likes a spot away from blasting winds and frost pockets, and will appreciate the protected environment of an urban garden. The leaves, as they unfurl in spring, are the most delicate green – they look almost too fragile to stay on the plant. *A. palmatum* 'Sango-Kaku' (syn. *A. p.* 'Senkaki') has coral red branches and shoots, and its new leaves are edged with red. In summer the leaves are all green, providing quite a dense canopy, but in the autumn they start to turn, eventually becoming golden yellow, tinged with red. Just before leaf fall a decent-sized tree resembles a giant golden torch. In winter sun, the colour of the red bark, which does not peel, seems to positively glow. This is a slow grower and makes a good container plant. To stop the leaf edges from browning, site it out of direct sun and strong winds.

Arudinaria nitida (syn. Fargesia nitida)

Arundinaria nitida is one of my favourite specimen bamboos. It looks stunning and it's also easy going and adaptable. It's completely hardy, grows happily to 4m/12ft high, forms neat clumps without becoming invasive, doesn't mind the wind too much (a problem with many bamboos), and is remarkably pollution tolerant. It likes a sheltered site where the soil retains moisture, and where it gets full sun to dappled shade, but it will survive in dry soils, and deeper shade. It will even tolerate exposed locations (but the wind will strip off most of its leaves over winter). This bamboo is also an excellent tub plant but you will have to divide it every few years as it outgrows its space. Bamboos look stunning against brickwork and/or water: it's the perfect marriage of hard and soft landscaping. In a mixed planting give it room to form clumps, and put it with rounded shapes and pale greens, such as *Euphorbia mellifera* or *Choisya ternata* 'Sundance'.

Blechnum spicant

As its common name suggests, the 'hard fern' is a tough little evergreen plant ideal for small gardens, growing to a height and spread of 30–75cm/12–30in. Blechnum is fully hardy and like many ferns prefers a damp soil in a shady position. An acidic, peaty soil is preferable, with plenty of organic matter. Blechnum is good for urban environments as it tolerates both strong winds and air pollution. It's great for jungle themes and just the thing for mass ground-cover planting, or for stuffing individually into pockets within decaying walls. However it's also perfect for containers – both planted in isolation, or with bedding plants – where its leathery, spreading, dark green fronds flatter showy plants like geraniums. Blechnum is a multi-functional plant, suited to most designs and thriving in conditions where many other plants would struggle. To keep it looking good, regularly remove fading fronds near to the base. It'll encourage new green shoots and prevent the plant from looking straggly and unkempt. That; and a regular mulching of good compost, is all that's required.

Chimonanthus praecox

This twiggy, deciduous shrub is hardly a star performer for most of the year, yet it's still one of my favourites. At the gloomiest point of winter, when nothing seems to be happening, this plant slips in quietly from the wings and steals the show, hence it's common name, wintersweet. Small, translucent, yellow bell-shaped flowers form on bare twigs, with a texture like transparent lemon sherbet. In frosty weather, these hang like tiny, yellow glass lanterns. Get close and the scent from these is piercingly sweet, such a wonderful shock on a miserable winter's day. Being a classic primadonna, the wintersweet only flowers well where it's happy, and sometimes takes a few years to bloom. But it's worth the wait. Choice, expensive and classy, it's a must for a south-facing or west-facing aspect, growing slowly over the years to reach an eventual height of 3m/10ft. To cover its summer drabness, run a large-flowered clematis through it. It can be successfully container grown, but prefers being planted out.

Clematis armandii 'Apple Blossom'

All clematis do a first-class job of providing screening and privacy in the garden, but most species are deciduous and lose their leaves over winter. *Clematis armandii* is evergreen and looks good all year round. Its leaves are different from other species, too: long and lance-like, they appear as dark green fingers. When it flowers, early in the year, the almond scent of its white flowers fills the spring garden. *C. armandii* has a reputation for being difficult to grow; that's often because it has been planted in the wrong place, but it can be temperamentally tender in some areas. This choice climber needs a warm west wall to really give its all – don't plant it in a frost pocket. Like all clematis it's also a greedy feeder, doing best on good, humus-rich soil with its roots protected from hot sun. But I think it gives a much better flowering display when slightly starved. When happy it is far more vigorous than you would expect from a slightly temperamental subject, and will romp away to cover most structures.

Corylus avellana 'Contorta'

A hardy, deciduous, bushy relative of the common hazel or cobnut, ultimately reaching 4m/13ft in height and spread. Relatively slow growing, this plant is ideal for small urban gardens. It requires sun or semi-shade, and a well-drained fertile soil. Hazels will tolerate poor soils if lots of well-composted organic matter is incorporated when they are planted. Grown for its curious contorted stems (hence its common name: the corkscrew hazel), each branch is covered in sharply toothed leaves. In winter the naked branches bear pendulous pale yellow catkins which, when frosted, glisten like small tears. *Corylus avellana* 'Contorta' has a habit like nothing else (except perhaps the dragon's claw willow, *Salix matsudana* 'Tortuosa', which is much more vigorous). Ideal as a lone specimen plant, this hazel is equally at home within both traditional and modern planting schemes – a shrub perfectly suited to containers old and contemporary alike. If suckers occur, cut them out with a sharp saw as close to the point of origin as possible, or they will take over.

Crocosmia 'Lucifer'

Seldom was there a more fitting name for a plant; the herbaceous perennial 'Lucifer' produces flowers in a more hell-fire red than you can imagine! Originally from South Africa, this bulbous plant has a lot to recommend it. A real toughie, 3ft/1m tall, it fits in where a strong vertical accent is required, and the leaves, which appear before the flowers, are useful in their own right. Montbretia has been a garden stalwart for decades, even if familiarity made it sometimes overlooked, but this cultivar is very different to the common orange variety. Poor soils, dry soils, neglect – it can take them all, and will form satisfyingly large clumps over the years. The small flowers are carried on strong stems that tower over the sword-shaped foliage. When they flower the effect is dramatic, as the blooms open from the base to the tip, the process lasting a few weeks. Even when the flowers fall, the knobbly green immature seeds are interesting, and when these turn brown they make decorative seedheads through the winter.

Daphne odora 'Aureomarginata'

You must grow this queen of scent! Once you smell the powerful fragrance in spring – filling the air for several metres around – you'll become a daphne addict, too! For me, there is no better plant. Forming a loose, rounded shape eventually some 1.5m/5ft in height and with a similar spread, this is a choice plant for a south or south-west aspect. It is not fully hardy but the cosy city microclimate will help enormously. *D. odora* 'Aureomarginata', with yellow-edged leaves, is hardier, and will survive all but the worst winters, so if you're worried, grow that instead. Its small, neat, evergreen leaves carry it though the year, but in spring the pinky-white flower clusters open, and the scent takes over the entire garden. Plant it against a front wall and you'll have people banging on your door to ask you what the plant is; no-one can ignore the sweet fragrance. Daphnes hate root disturbance and appreciate a well-drained but retentive soil, with a compost mulch. They can be grown in large, sheltered pots and are best in full sun.

Euphorbia mellifera

GOOD

Perfect for a sunny spot in a sheltered garden, this is a large, choice semi-evergreen shrub that can reach 2m/6ft in height and spread, and has a neat, rounded shape. It's an architectural diva – as are all the euphorbias – but this one has something extra: a fine scent. In spring, huge sticky flower clusters open and fill the air with a sweet, honeyed fragrance. The leaves are almost apple green – paler than those on its better-known cousin, *E. characias* – and it's slightly more delicate, too. Frost will make the leaves droop alarmingly and bad winter weather will cause it to lose a few, so if severe frosts are forecast, cover it with fleece. Although really bad weather will kill it, it should survive in protected urban gardens. Site *E. mellifera* with care in a well-drained spot, and give it room to fill out its allotted space – this is one plant you can't squeeze in, or you risk spoiling the shape. *E. mellifera* has shallow roots and is not invasive, though if it's happy you may find seedlings spread over the garden. It looks great in gravelled planting schemes with phormiums, perhaps, and bergenias tucked in at its feet.

Fatsia japonica

GOOD

Large, dark green palmate leaves give the fatsia immediate presence. The evergreen leaf surfaces of this large, useful shrub are glossy and reflect light. As a backbone shrub against a fence or a wall it stands alone, needing no accompaniment. Although it happily thrives outside, fatsia's other role is as a houseplant, but it often grows too big for its space (3m/10ft height and spread). Commonly known as the Japanese aralia, it's an excellent subject for a shady courtyard or an area adjacent to the house. Its slightly exotic air means it fits very well into modern planting schemes. You can't plant it next to the cottage garden flowers – the two just don't hit it off – but among the unusual and similarly dramatic it holds its own beautifully. Any soil will suit as long as it isn't waterlogged. Fatsia can take drought well when it's old, and it does equally well in sun or shade, though don't site it in a hot summer area as its talents will be wasted. Shady enclosures are its domain. An excellent courtyard or terrace plant.

Laurus nobilis

GOOD

In warm climates the sweet bay is a sizeable evergreen tree. I have seen specimens in the west country of over 6m/18ft, but that is unusual. Mediterranean in origin, the sweet bay likes the sun and heat – and small plants are more vulnerable than established ones, so they do particularly well with a warm wall behind them. The bay is attractive even as a juvenile, with its small neat leaves and its tiny, scented creamy flowers. Bay is an excellent plant for urban gardeners because of its adaptability. Slow growing, its size can be restricted with ease, and the foliage is ideal for clipping into shapes. The ball-headed bay trees either side of a front door are a common sight – here, one stem is selected and allowed to form a standard. Apart from being a good backbone piece of architecture, you can use the leaves, fresh or dried, in the kitchen. Ordinary well-drained soil will satisfy bay trees, and they look superb in containers. They will even tolerate dry conditions. When young, protect from severe frosts and wind.

Lavandula stoechas

If you like the smell of lavender but want a more stylish and altogether more interesting plant, the French lavender is the one to plump for. This is the upstart among the lavender family, with cheeky flowers borne on straight stems. The flower resembles a deep, lavender-purple raspberry with Mickey Mouse ears(!) and is startlingly different from the ordinary English lavender (*Lavandula angustifolia*). I think it makes a rather more modern statement; the flowers certainly stand out with their notable eccentricity and are often a cause for comment. The leaves are finely cut, too, suggesting a more noble pedigree. But there is a price to pay for such individual character – the plant is not as tough as its English cousin. Harsh winter frosts, or an open aspect where it takes the full force of an east wind, will kill it. As an excellent pot subject it can be moved to the most sheltered part of the garden, or even taken inside the greenhouse. Looks great among Mediterranean plants in a sunny, well-drained soil, but it's also useful for marking the side of a path and in naturalistic plantings.

Lilium regale

With so many lilies to choose from it was hard to pick one! I've chosen this because I think it's the easiest and most rewarding to grow. Most lilies are fabulous, some can be quite temperamental customers, but the regal lily is solid and dependable. Pick the biggest bulbs when they are on sale in the nursery, and plant deeply, straight away, in a well-drained, compost-rich soil. I'd automatically plant them in a pot – in the garden they also do well, but can be prone to rotting in wet weather, and being eaten by slugs. As pot-queens they look superb and their flowers add dramatic impact wherever planted. And what flowers! From claret-red buds 10cm/4in long, they open out into huge, white blooms with golden stamens, pumping out scent, especially in the late afternoon and evening. One pot of lilies in flower and brought indoors will scent out the entire house! Although you'll get 6–30 large flowers per strong upright stem, these bulbs look best in groups. They like sun but will last longer in light shade.

Malus 'Evereste'

A small, deciduous tree ultimately reaching 3.5m/11ft in height, *Malus* 'Evereste' is ideal for small gardens. It works hard for its place, flowering more profusely than any other crab apple. Pink in bud, the flowers open white in spring, and ultimately carpet the ground underneath like snowflakes. Long-lasting yellow fruits, with a red cheek, follow in late summer/early autumn. It will grow anywhere except in deep shade and a waterlogged soil, where diseases can become a problem. *Malus* 'Evereste' offers more resistance to disease than the red-flowering forms, such as *M.* 'Red Glow', and its more common yellow-fruiting cousin, *M.* 'Golden Hornet'. Like many trees, crab apples need a small stake for support, especially when laden with fruit. Avoid siting it in a windy spot, or your flowers and fruit will end up next door! It is perfect for containers, as its roots aren't particularly prolific, but don't grow it on a patio where squashed fruit may act like the proverbial banana skin. Do collect the edible fruits though.

Pittosporum tobira

The Japanese pittosporum is a delight among spring-flowering shrubs. The flowers sit nicely in the middle of a whorl of glossy evergreen leaves in a large creamy white cluster, and last from spring through to summer. The flowers fade to cream, then to light yellow, before dropping. Their scent is a mix of orange blossom and fruit, and on warm days the plant sends out blasts of this heady fragrance. It relishes a warm microclimate and the protection many enclosed urban gardens can give. In a hard winter, however, it's worth wrapping the plant in horticultural fleece, just to be on the safe side. But always give it your most sheltered, warmest spot. It likes well-drained soil in full sun, so it's an ideal subject for a south or south-west aspect, especially if it's protected from biting winds by other tall plants nearby, or ideally grown against a wall. Once established, pittosporum tolerates drought well. Again, if you site the plant right, it will be one to be proud of. It's slow to get to its eventual height of around 2m/6ft and so can be grown in a large tub.

Trachelospermum jasminoides

I like the common name 'star jasmine' for this climber, so suited to enclosed urban spaces. The pure white, six-petalled flowers bloom in high summer and they do look like stars, or little cartwheels. An evergreen with small, dark leaves, it likes to be grown in good soil against a sunny wall; it hates wind, which will cause the leaves to discolour and the plant to ail. Give it a sheltered spot in fertile soil – this is one plant which repays cosseting in its early years. Its main joy is the sweet-fruit scent, which is quite addictive. In a wind-still place this will waft gently around a seating area. Not vigorous like clematis, this plant twines slowly and may need a bit of help tying in the shoots. Don't prune: it flowers on old wood, and it's seldom necessary anyway. It's a slow starter and needs the right conditions to perform well. It can be grown successfully in a container; slightly pot-bound specimens have been know to flower better, but you do have to keep your eyes on this fussy madam. Train it over trellis, or over an arch by a seat.

Verbena bonariensis

Beloved of National Trust gardens and those with room for sweeping borders, this stately herbaceous perennial also adds a dash of finesse to urban planting schemes. It has the kind of good breeding which makes it socialise well with others and yet makes a classic, individual statement, too. It's a trendy customer, and expensive because of it, but can be grown easily from seed when it will flower a year after sowing, going on to bulk up nicely in subsequent seasons to form a handsome and airy clump. It likes sun, is not fussy about soil, and can tolerate some exposure. The neat, square, wiry stems rise vertically to 1.5m/5ft in height and branch out delicately into small lavender-purple flower clusters with a final top-knot. Plant together in a bold clump about 10cm/4in apart. For longevity in the late-summer garden, this verbena can't be beaten: it will keep going in good conditions until the frosts hit. If winter is very severe, some straw mulch protection is a good idea, but urban gardens should be trouble-free.

BAD

Many of these plants I do genuinely love – honest! Some have fantastic shape, some have brilliant colours, but, I'm afraid, all of them raise difficulties for small urban gardens. Often it's due to their rapid growth or size so I've tried to suggest alternatives.

Betula utilis var *jacquemontii*

Birches are perhaps our most valuable trees, providing interest all year round. Some are suited to urban gardens, although many are strong growers exceeding 10m/33ft or more. A notable exception is Young's weeping birch (*Betula pendula* 'Youngii), a small weeping dome-shaped tree that won't top 8m/26ft in height and width. This particular deciduous West Himalayan birch, like many of its kind, is grown for its glorious paper-thin, creamy-white, peeling bark, and its golden yellow autumn colour. It is upright – unlike its pendulous cousin, the common silver birch (*Betula pendula*) – and is commonly available. Its shape when young, however, is somewhat bulbous – fatter at the base than the top. This is unfortunate. Where space is limited, fat bulbous trees only accentuate the size of a small garden because the soil beneath cannot be used for additional planting.

Buddleja davidii varieties

Buddleja davidii has got a bad reputation. It grows anywhere, from the most polluted railway siding to garden walls – the magpie of the plant world, it sees a space somewhere, and goes right in. Its infamy is unjustified, though, for buddleja is a magnificent deciduous shrub, called the 'butterfly bush' because its flower spikes attract butterflies, as well as bees and other insects, like no other. In summer, long tubular scented flowers adorn arching stems, which in turn are covered by long, lance-shaped dark green leaves with white felted undersides. As tough as old boots, *Buddleja davidii* cultivars tolerate very low temperatures and extreme air pollution, and will easily grow to 5m/16ft in height and spread, so aren't ideal for the smaller urban garden. Even in larger gardens they must be placed carefully, ideally next to evergreens at the back of large borders where they can grow to their full glory.

Delphinium – large-flowered hybrids

The most common delphiniums are the large-flowered garden hybrids, descending from *Delphinium elatum*. Grown for their tall spikes of irregular cup-shaped flowers, celebrated varieties include the violet-flowered 'Chelsea Star', 'Blue Dawn' and the silvery mauve 'Fanfare'. Stately plants, colours are available to suit any planting scheme, and in mid-summer there is no better traditional cottage-garden favourite. They also, strangely, tolerate air pollution. Unfortunately, however, all delphiniums are fussy and require full sun and a good, nutrient-rich, moisture-retentive soil. The large-flowered garden hybrids also need staking to prevent them breaking under their own weight, especially as some grow to 2m/6ft in height. Delphiniums also need regular feeding and watering throughout spring and summer; they're attention seekers and require looking after. So think carefully: can you give them the time and effort they deserve?

Dicksonia antarctica

Commonly known as the tree fern, *Dicksonia antarctica* originates from Australia. It's a valuable shade-lover, requiring a sheltered site and humus-rich, moist soil. Like many other plants deriving from hotter climates, it's frost tender and should be protected in particularly cold weather; straw stuffed and tied into the top of its bristly trunk, where the palm-like fronds originate, should insulate it suitably. This fern will grow to more than 10m/33ft in height, but typically only half that in temperate climates. Tree ferns work best under trees or in wooded glades where they'll receive dappled sunlight, and are ideal planted in conjunction with other shade-loving ferns such as *Osmunda regalis* (royal fern) or lush hostas. Tree ferns have become very trendy in recent years; they look exotic, and every fashionista has one. However, initially they cost a fortune, they are fussy about their environment, and require continual attention and a watchful eye. They're a plant suited to those with time and some knowledge – not for the time-strapped beginner. But if you are prepared to nurture it, you won't be disappointed.

Eucalyptus gunnii

Few more attractive specimen trees, the cider gum is also perfectly suited to green and white planting schemes. Grown for its peeling cream and brown bark, and aromatic silver-blue foliage, eucalyptus will very quickly become an evergreen single-stemmed monster reaching 25m/82ft in height if not pruned severely. As well as controlling its size, annual pruning will also encourage new rounded leaves, whereas, if left unpruned, the old leaves fade and become large, green and leathery. *Eucalyptus gunnii* is probably the hardiest of the species; however, it still dislikes temperatures below zero, so needs planting in a sunny position. It is drought tolerant, and therefore doesn't need regular watering, but it does require a well-drained, fertile soil. Gum trees are generally not for the small garden because they have an aggressive root system and will play havoc with foundations and footings if planted close to buildings. *Eucalyptus niphophila* is an exception, though you'll still need to keep its growth in check.

Gunnera manicata

Looking like giant rhubarb, gunnera is an architectural gem. An enormous clump-forming herbaceous perennial with vast, bristly lobed leaves over 2m/6ft across, it requires a wet boggy site in full sun. Ideally, it should be planted next to water or on marshy ground. Like the leaves, the flowers are breathtaking: long, prehistoric-looking, light green spikes which in early summer arch out like giant stubbly rockets from the centre of the plant. These are followed by orangey seedpods, which are again architecturally unique. Gunnera is only frost hardy, so it will require protection from low temperatures, and it doesn't like strong winds. Cover the crowns in winter with the old giant leaves and straw for insulation. Gunnera is a horticultural oddity, and worthy of the highest praise. It's a gob-smacker, but don't be tempted unless you have the space! Its size has to be seen to be believed, and it's a greedy, attention-seeking beast, too, requiring a fair degree of care.

Lavatera

Like buddleja, the tree mallow has its critics, primarily because of its vigorous nature. This deciduous shrub will easily reach 2m/6ft in height and spread within a year, and due to this sappy growth it often needs staking. Fortunately, lavatera loves a hard prune – just as well because you'll need to attack it a couple of times during the year to curb its ever-increasing size. It prefers a sunny position, so ensure it's not sited in a cold and exposed place. A south- or west-facing wall is ideal. The pale pink *Lavatera olbia* 'Rosea' is by far the most common variety available. However the pinkish-white 'Barnsley', which also has a red eye, and the purplish-red 'Burgundy Wine', are also popular. Lavatera is a back-of-the-border plant. Given enough room its arching branches will be covered in large hollyhock-like flowers that'll last from mid-summer through to late autumn. A visual treat when its flowers cascade through evergreens such *Viburnum tinus* and *Prunus laurocerasus* 'Otto Luyken', lavatera must be given space, and therefore it's a poor choice in very small gardens.

Liquidambar styraciflua

The sweet gums are one of the most glorious hardy ornamental trees in the world. With a leaf shape reminiscent of *Acer palmatum* (Japanese maple), their autumn colour is nothing short of spectacular, turning from green to orange, purple and red in autumn. *Liquidambar styraciflua* 'Lane Roberts' and 'Worplesdon' are noted varieties, both turning a deep reddish purple colour. All liquidambars prefer a fertile soil but will usually grow happily on anything except shallow chalk. All prefer sun or semi-shade. Their broadly conical shape is stunningly simple and shows off the foliage beautifully. Unfortunately *Liquidambar styraciflua* and its varieties are not small garden trees. They'll ultimately reach a height of 25m/82ft and a spread of 12m/40ft. Choose instead the oriental sweet gum (*Liquidambar orientalis*), a slow-growing, smaller version which reaches only 6m/20ft, spread 4m/12ft – a suitable substitute with similar attributes. However, it will never quite eclipse the autumn colour of 'Worplesdon'.

Parthenocissus tricuspidata

The Boston or Japanese ivy is a woody-stemmed climber ideal for shady north- and east-facing walls, and is tolerant of pollution as well as poor soil. Unlike clematis and jasmine, parthenocissus won't need any additional support. Using tendrils tipped with sucker-like pads, it'll free-climb walls and fences of its own accord, making it ideal for covering large expanses of wall. Grown for its broad, trident-shaped leaves, which turn from green to a brilliant crimson red in autumn, these are nothing short of spectacular. Planted next to large trees the effect is accentuated, resembling a tall pillar of vibrant colour. Parthenocissus is a tidy plant, and not particularly invasive, but it is very fast growing, reaching 20m/65ft and so it needs plenty of space, otherwise its autumn colour is wasted. Like other free-climbing plants it will cause damage to dated or already poor brickwork, dislodging mortar and enhancing small fissures. It's not as destructive as some climbers, such as common ivy, but it is one to watch.

Pyracantha

These fully hardy evergreen shrubs are grown for their clusters of early summer white flowers and round orange, red or yellow autumn berries. Commonly known as 'firethorn', pyracantha requires a sheltered site, ideally against a south- or west-facing wall. A fertile, free-draining soil is preferable. The narrow leaves are dark green and glossy, and when grown against a fence or wall provide a perfect backdrop to showy herbaceous perennials. Most will need plenty of space, as these vigorous plants will easily reach a height and spread of 5m/16ft. The dwarf form is 'Red Cushion', growing to approximately 1m/3ft high. Most pyracanthas, such as the commonly available 'Golden Charmer' and 'Orange Glow', are good for perimeter hedging as they have long, sharp spines that will deter intruders. But because of their aggressive nature it's unwise to plant firethorn near children's areas; these brutes will puncture footballs and tender skin alike. Unfortunately, most varieties are also susceptible to scab and fire-blight – except for the American hybrids such as 'Mohave' or 'Teton'.

Salix 'Chrysocoma'

The majestic deciduous golden weeping willow is famed for its slender yellow shoots and yellow-green leaves which droop like a dense curtain. Its yellow stems look positively vibrant in late winter, standing proud in many parks and large gardens, when other trees only look grey and dreary. This broadly spreading classic is only for the largest urban garden, as it's as wide as it is tall – anything up to 25m/82ft. Coupled with a dense canopy, like all large willows, it's very fast growing with a root system to match, sucking any water or nutrients from the soil for some distance around. Only the toughest plants can compete and grow happily in close proximity. Prone to fungal diseases resulting in stem cankers, weeping willows are also susceptible to infestations of caterpillars and aphids. It acts as a beacon, encouraging pests to chew on all the other delicacies nearby. Leave this tree in the park, it's not for typical urban gardens, and it's liable to cause problems with shade, fallen debris and nearby buildings.

Wisteria sinensis

Seldom does a climber flower so profusely. In early summer racemes of purple-blue flowers cascade from this deciduous woody-stemmed plant like a waterfall. The pea-like flowers are highly fragrant and, if grown next to a house, the pungent scent will fill every room. Requiring full sun and fertile soil, all wisterias need support, be it trellis or a wire system, and must be tied in and pruned regularly, once in spring and again in summer. Vigorous growers, they'll easily get out of control if left alone, particularly the most rampant *Wisteria sinensis*. Untouched, it'll grow to more than 30m/100ft – not something you want tied to the side of a house. The Japanese wisteria (*Wisteria floribunda*) is far less rampant, only growing to 9m/30ft, and makes a much better choice for training over arches, pergolas or against buildings. The flowers are also larger, 60cm/2ft long as opposed to 30cm/1ft. *Wisteria floribunda* 'Alba' is a stunning white-flowered variety which is perfect for an urban, sunny wall.

UGLY

Acer pseudoplatanus 'Brilliantissimum'

As you've guessed, trees are my obsession, and maples in particular are a delight. Many, like *Acer cappadocicum* and *Acer maximowiczianum*, have incredibly brilliant autumn colour and some, such as *Acer rufinerve*, are noted for their bark. I would even go so far to say that the Japanese maples (*Acer palmatum* varieties) make my top five. However, *Acer pseudoplatanus* 'Brilliantissimum' wouldn't even get a rating. Why? Because of its young salmon-pink leaves. Now I'm not averse to garish colour. In fact, bright eye-socking colour is sometimes exactly what I want. But garish salmon pink is just too much. This tree should be driving an old Capri, wearing white socks and slip-on shoes. It's a clichéd poser, and detracts from more versatile plants underneath. Thank goodness the leaves eventually yellow, and ultimately turn dark green. It is slow-growing and suited for small gardens but be careful of this one – that salmon pink positively screams.

Cortaderia selloana

There is nothing like pampas grass to instigate passionate debate. In one camp are those who embrace this stately evergreen grass, and there are others like me who wish it were in the circus as a freak. It's a fairly well behaved clump-former, but impractical for an urban garden: I've seen them stretch out to over 3m/10ft in width. Admittedly, in late summer it bears tall erect plumes of flowers but for the rest of the year the lacklustre mid-green leaves act like razor blades ready to cut the unsuspecting gardener to shreds. It's popular because people are seduced by its initial size and the prospect of dramatic impact. But just how much drama do you want? Plant it in a sunny position and it'll soon take over. To check its size, cortaderia should really be carefully set on fire – honest! (Which is actually the only enjoyable thing about this plant: you can burn it – heh!) Pick another grass and leave this 'sixties surburban fashion fad at the garden centre.

x Cupressocyparis leylandii

A vigorous upright conifer, x *Cupressocyparis leylandii* is now probably the most popular hedging plant in the UK. It grows fast fast fassst!, satisfying our demand for instant gardening. Look down any street and you'll find it: a big, fat, dense green blob. No autumn colour, no attractive seeds, no attractive bark, no flowers. This plant was spawned by the devil himself! To control it you need the patience of a saint, plus a couple of large brandies, because it needs regular trimming to restrict a potentially enormous size. Unchecked, it'll easily grow to 30m/100ft. It craves full sun, but does absolutely nothing to deserve such a prime position. Your neighbours will hate you for growing a plant that blocks out all the sun. And don't think that by purchasing the golden form it'll look any more stylish; it'll only advertise still further that you've plumped for one of the most mediocre and bland hedging plants available. It really should be banned!

Fraxinus excelsior

A vigorous, deciduous, spreading tree reaching 30m/100ft in height and spread, the common ash is totally unsuitable for urban gardens. Like the sycamore, this tree is a prolific seeder, and will grow practically anywhere except on very dry soils. In small gardens seedlings should be identified and removed quickly, otherwise they will grow rapidly, drowning out other plants, and transforming themselves into hulking great monsters. Everything about this native tree is a let-down. Its dull green leaves don't appear until very late, its flowers are insignificant, the bark is nothing to write home about, and its shape – unlike *Fraxinus oxycarpa* 'Raywood' and the elegant narrow-leaved *Fraxinus angustifolia* – is disorganised and messy. Even its autumn colour is poor: a dull insipid yellow, if you're lucky. And its leaves are not only the last to form, they're the first to drop! Ash should not be grown near buildings or communal areas as it has very brittle branches which break easily under strong winds or heavy snowfall. This tree is best left in the wild where it has the space it needs.

Fremontodendron californicum

The flannel flower is so overrated it's infuriating. Everybody goes on about what a spectacular wall shrub it is. Rubbish! It's fussy and belligerent. Ultimately growing to a height and spread of 5m/16ft, it needs a south- or west-facing wall, otherwise it's too chicken to survive the winter. Fremontodendron is also particularly fussy about soil: only the best free-draining stuff will do; otherwise it won't last long, nor will it produce many of its only asset, those large saucer-shaped yellow flowers. It'll need a stake when young (preferably through the heart!), and, unlike many plants, fremontodendron resents being moved, so plant it carefully. If you've made a mistake and planted it in the wrong place, purchase another and don't try to move it as chances are it'll poke the finger at you and die. To top it all, the flannel flower will cause a nasty itchy rash if you come into close contact. A real pain as it's quite vigorous, and therefore needs a regular prune to manage its size. No way!

Ligustrum ovalifolium 'Aureum'

Privet is a common evergreen hedging shrub, used widely in cities and by the sea because of its pollution- and salt-tolerance. It's a fast grower, and will form a dense hedge if clipped regularly to control its size. So why attack this bastion of horticulture? Well, the yellow variegated leaves are monotonous, its insignificant black berries are poisonous, and the fragrance? Yuck! The tubular white flowers, which appear in summer, smell like a public toilet – not something I'd like bordering my property! There are so many other better alternatives: evergreens such as elaeagnus, griselinia, osmanthus, *Prunus laurocerasus* (cherry laurel) and my personal favourite *Pittosporum tenuifolium*, with its glossy green leaves, purple stems and honey-scented flowers. All are commonly available, easy to trim into formal geometric hedges, and are far more aesthetically pleasing. The old saying, 'familiarity breeds contempt', applies to privet, and rightly so: it's unadventurous and boring. Pick something else, and stand out from the crowd.

Polygonum baldschuanicum

Every urban garden needs a climber to provide height in a design and to screen an unsightly boundary, but stay well away from this vigorous nightmare. Russian vine, or the mile-a-minute plant, is one of the fastest-growing climbers available, and will easily grow to 12m/40ft in a few years. It almost grows too fast for itself, so you rarely have a chance to see its delicate panicles of pink or white flowers which appear in summer and autumn. The plant reaches straight for the heavens leaving straggly, unattractive woody stems on show, and lofting the flowers out of sight. That's assuming you haven't already chopped it down by then! Like most vigorous plants it competes with your lovelies for water and nutrients, and if planted near a tree it'll hitch a ride, twine its way up, and like a boa constrictor squeeze your statuesque specimen to death. I'd tolerate this climber if it were more showy, but *Parthenocissus tricuspidata* (Boston ivy) is a better choice – at least its spectacular crimson autumn colour makes its rampancy almost tolerable.

Rhus typhina

This plant will try to convince you it's worthy of any garden, but don't let it deceive you – this one's a criminal! A deciduous large shrub or small tree (height and spread 5m/16ft) *Rhus typhina* has attractive fern-like, pinnate foliage which cloaks the velvety new shoots. In autumn the dark green leaves turn brilliant orange, accompanied by deep red fruit clusters. But the downside is that rhus has a behaviour problem, sending out foraging roots to colonise any uncharted soil within the garden. It does what it wants, and you'll never curb its invasive root system. Disease resistance is also awful, and mature specimens are usually riddled with coral spot or heartwood decay, for which there's no satisfactory control. While reasonably hardy, a severe frost may kill it, so a sunny position is a must. Its general demeanour reminds me of a smoky old gentlemen's club – brown and dirty, with old velveteen sofas covered in dust and unmentionables.

Scentless roses

Until recently, roses were consistently voted the nation's favourite plant, so I'll tread carefully here. I only dislike those without a beautiful fragrance. Many new modern hybrid tea (large-flowered roses) and floribunda (cluster-flowered roses) introductions are devoid of scent. They're bred for flower colour alone, and scent doesn't get a look in. What a cheat! Everyone bends to sniff a rose so what an anticlimax if there is no scent! Old garden roses (Damask, Bourbon, Gallica, Alba) and simple species roses like *Rosa rugosa* are among the most fragrant roses, and are therefore a much better choice than those scentless ones... although there are obviously exceptions. Species and old roses don't require so much pruning, they often produce better hips, and are also particularly pest and disease resistant; whereas modern roses tend to be clobbered by aphids, black spot, powdery mildew and rust. Species roses are also the most tolerant – liking almost all soils and making excellent spiny hedges

Symphoricarpus albus

Isn't it a bit unfair to poke fun at this inoffensive arching shrub? Why not pick on meatier plants with offensive dispositions, and leave this waiting-in-the cupboard plant alone? Well, I guess it's all right if mediocrity is your thing, but as a garden-worthy plant the snowberry should have been given its exit visa long ago. It never looks right wherever it's planted. It never seems to look healthy, either. Imagine a scrawny set of twigs arching feebly out of a clump, with sparse leaves of no merit whatsoever tacked onto the stems, and you'll get the picture. Snowberry sounds fun, you may say. What? A few round white berries (and I mean a few – this plant is so mean it has my nickname of the 'grudge plant'). And that's it, folks! Wherever I see this waster of good garden space I want to rip it out... apart from winter hedges in the countryside, where its spindly nature somehow makes its bland character blend in, even if it's not a shining asset. What would happen if a specimen was fed luxuriously and cosseted like other plants? Would I be impressed? Afraid not – it's simply not worthy of space.

Viburnum rhytidophyllum

Viburnums are an enormously diverse and valuable group of plants. Among them are both evergreen and deciduous beauties, renowned for their shape, fruit, flower and scent. The scented ones especially are fantastic in the spring garden with showy, highly-scented white or pink blooms. But watch out for this wolf in sheep's clothing; it gives its beautiful compatriots a bad name. A vigorous, broadly-spreading beast, *Viburnum rhytidophyllum* can achieve a height and spread of 4m/12ft. Its long leaves are dark green, and covered in a dull white down which many people find irritates their skin. The plant actually looks dirty, as though it's recently been spat from an enormous exhaust pipe! Perhaps that's why it tolerates pollution so well. The flowers, which appear in spring, are a dreary creamy white, and epitomise the dull personality of this plant. *Viburnum rhytidophyllum* is a garden nasty, and doesn't care who knows it. Not a plant for the discerning urban gardener.

Yucca gloriosa 'Variegata'

If you want to frighten people off, choose this feral monster of a plant. Commonly named the Spanish dagger, it's like a tank and can take just about everything you'd want to throw at it! Sure, it's architectural, with its immensely tough huge pointed leaves and vast spilling crown. In fact it's so dominant, it's dangerous: it will send out a hit squad at night to get rid of all its near-neighbours. If you get too close, or threaten it with the chop, it'll jab you viciously and sneakily with the most horrendous thorns on the tips of its leaves that you'll run away and wonder if you should pay it protection money! These spines are unaccountably nasty, as strong as an iron needle, and they go in with malicious precision. Not a plant to include if you have children or pets, this is X-rated material which belongs well away from lawns (you're sure to impale yourself when you're mowing round it) or paths. It does look spectacular in a gravel bed, all by itself. It's a growling anti-social beast, and sleeps alone, thank you.

INDEX

MANY THANKS TO THE FOLLOWING:

My family who have supported me no end throughout my career in horticulture (especially my dad, mum and Lina for putting me on the right tracks).

All at my publishers, HarperCollinsPublishers especially the team in Home and Garden Reference.

All the chaps at Two Four Productions (and Cine Wessex) who worked so hard to produce the television programme, through sometimes difficult and tricky circumstances. We had a laugh though, didn't we?!

Everyone at Channel Four who have supported the City Gardener project so magnificently.

My agents at Curtis Brown, Julian and Ali, not forgetting Viv and Jane.

Many thanks to North East Surrey College of Technology (NESCOT) for their continued support, especially my colleagues in the horticulture department.

Flittons Nursery and Plant Centre and Tendercare Nurseries for some of the best plants I've ever seen.

Last, but definitely not least, my friends — especially Tom and James. Without whom none of this would have been possible. Thanks, dudes!

THE PUBLISHERS WOULD LIKE TO THANK:

Nikki English, Tim Sandall, Julia McCabe, Iain MacDonald, Annabel Hibbard and Gill Hennessey
at Two Four Productions and Channel Four.

The following locations used in photography:

Chumleigh Gardens, Burgess Park, SE5

Flittons Nursery & Plant Centre, Woodmansterne Lane, Wallington, SM6

Geffrye Museum, Kingsland Road, London, E2

The Museum of Garden History, Lambeth Palace Road, London, SE1

The Roof Gardens, 99 Kensington High Street, London W8

And
Fulham Palace Garden Centre, Bishops Avenue, SW6 – and also for supplying props.
All profits from the garden centre go to the charity Fairbridge, which supports inner city youth.

FURTHER READING

RHS Encyclopaedia of Gardening, (1992) Dorling Kindersley
A horticultural bible, loads of pictures, practical step by steps, how tos, and simple explanations. A great reference book, if you only buy one other gardening book make it this one.

What Plant Where & *What Perennial Where*, Roy Lancaster (1995 &1997) Dorling Kindersley
Detailed books featuring plants for every area of your garden, in a simple to read format. Perfect for those just starting out.

Soil Care and Management, Jo Readman (1991) HDRA/ Search Press
A book ideal for beginners and experienced gardeners alike, loads of pictures, diagrams and fantastically simple explanations. Everything the gardener needs to know about the brown stuff.

Hardscape, Ann-Marie Powell, (2001) David & Charles Publishers
A visual treat. Loads of hard landscaping discussed including uses, suppliers and little construction techniques.

Really Small Gardens, Jill Billington (2002) Quadrille
A great little inspirational and instructive book for those with 'really small gardens'.

Rosemary Verey's Garden Plans, Rosemary Verey, (2001) Frances Lincoln Publishers
A plant book, by renowned plantswoman Rosemary Verey featuring ideas for planting schemes and garden designs alike.

PICTURE CREDITS